# If I Can Do It, You Can, Too!

A holistic approach to selling… attitudes and practices, necessities and enhancements, techniques and encouragements

## Scott S. Paterick

If I Can Do It, You Can, Too!
©2021, Scott S. Paterick

ISBN: 978-1-09839-293-2
ISBN eBook: 978-1-09839-294-9

This book is dedicated to my family and to my mentors in business....
Without them I would not have built a successful career.

# Foreword

This book is a must read for anyone in sales with a desire to improve their ability to serve their clients and reach higher levels of success. The reach of the book is broad but the advice is targeted and specific.

I've known Scott for over three decades. When I met him, he was a young single guy new to our industry. He had overcome some significant obstacles in his life and had a can-do attitude, but he was a raw rookie. Now Scott is a mature family man and a consistent top-producing veteran.

As he says in this book, there was no "magic" to attaining the success he has realized. I was always impressed with his thirst for knowledge and desire to improve his craft. And the real key was that he applied what he learned from others. It has been a great pleasure to watch Scott grow as a person and a professional. And as he says, "If he can do it, you can, too."

What I like most about this book is that it's not gimmicky. It describes common sense holistic methods of succeeding in sales. Scott does make a couple key assumptions about his readers, namely, that they have a passion for their business and a genuine desire to help others. If you have these two things, you can apply the processes and principles to achieve a high level of success.

This book offers some of the best insights from a top-flight producer and teacher. He presents straightforward descriptions of how to structure your business, attract potential clients and best serve existing ones. He emphasizes the necessity of honesty and a commitment to ethical practices. My hope is that as you read it you'll apply its ideas and principles to your life and profession to achieve the best for you and your family.

George R. Worley (CLU, ChFC, CLF)
Retired Chief Distribution and Marketing Officer,
Modern Woodmen of America

# CONTENTS

# Introduction

"I see." That's a phrase commonly used to indicate understanding of a situation or concept. For the first few years of my life, I couldn't honestly say those words. Poor vision drastically inhibited my ability to imagine or understand my world. From birth through the start of elementary school, seeing was a challenge. Initial diagnosis offered little promise of improvement and early trials of eyeglasses failed. My world seemed defined by my limits.

"I see." How much I wanted that to be my reality, to be the way I could experience my surroundings, to be a component of my social contacts.

When I entered school, I knew I was different from the other kids in my class and I sensed that in terms of social and intellectual development they were stages ahead of me. Fitting in and holding my own were not easy. Life, it seemed, would be a game of catch-up with prospects literally quite dim.

I'd had eye exams. I'd had that dismal experiment with glasses. Then one day, quite out of the blue, an ophthalmologist in town called my parents. "I know about your son," he said. "And I have an idea about what his condition is." At a hastily scheduled appointment, he described an unusual disorder and suggested doing a radical procedure that required choosing which eye to target for improvement and that involved, in effect, brain surgery. My mother chose the eye and both parents gave the go ahead.

So at age six, I had a rare and risky operation. Post-surgery, I was required to wear an eye patch for a couple months. It drove me crazy, and one day after a month of enduring it, I tore it off in a flash of impulsive disobedience. I did this in the kitchen of our home and recall the moment vividly. I saw, for the first time, the kitchen cabinets, a picture of the Last Supper with some dried palms, a porcelain bear cookie jar I had known only by the clink of its lid, and my mother. I remember saying: "Mom, so that's what you look like. And now I know where you hide the cookies." An immediate visit to the doctor determined, to the relief of all, that my eye-patch-snatch had not been detrimental.

Back at school, I could see. But I knew that my super-thick glasses made me "aesthetically different" and a target for continuing unkind teasing. And I knew, having missed much class time, that I was even further behind. Though the school pushed me through first and second grades, I was disconsolate at knowing I was the caboose on the academic train. I stated to my mother a despairing, "I'll never catch up." Her response was a life lesson in self-awareness, determination and goal-setting that I carry with me to this day. She said: "Don't compare yourself to others. Commit to working hard. You'll surpass others if you focus on your own goals."

I focused and I worked with persistence. By eighth grade, people in the school system began being surprised at my good test scores. I got moved into harder classes and thrived academically. And, after begging for contact lenses and saving toward their purchase, I finally got rid of the cumbersome glasses that I associated with cruel taunts, that I identified as a visible reminder of those difficult times when I could not say, "I see."

[A brief but important aside.... At age twelve I travelled to the Mayo Clinic where doctors confirmed what an outstanding job my ophthalmologist had done on a delicate and complicated surgical procedure. At twice that age, when I was a young businessman attending a luncheon meeting, I unexpectedly met the man who had operated on me and realized I had neither seen nor spoken to him for well over a decade. I determined to say what had long been in my heart. It was an emotional moment for me (and, seemingly, for him and for everyone else at our table). "Thank you," I said simply, "for my eyesight." Then I added, "How were we so lucky to find a doctor who had done this surgery?" He paused, and with what was a mixture of sheepishness, joy and utter forthrightness stated: "I had never done that surgery. That's not something I emphasized to your parents at the time. But I had studied and I knew the problem. I was secure in my diagnosis and in the scope of my abilities. I wanted to help. So I trusted in what I felt sure I could do." Those words taught me in a profound way how the confidence and vision of one person can – in this case quite literally – produce confidence and vision in another. I continually keep that in mind in my interactions with others.]

If you had told me in high school that I would some day have my own business, would have a deeply satisfying life, would achieve significant financial success, I probably would have laughed at you. But by the time I graduated high school, I'd acquired a great deal more knowledge than what had been provided by teachers and textbooks and tests. I had learned through experience some things that set the foundation of what I've built my life upon, things that form the basis for what I'll be sharing with you in this book. They were the valuable products of many, "I see," moments.

Right up front, I want to state four major takeaways from my experience. I'll refer back to these, sometimes overtly and sometimes subtly, in the pages ahead. In some ways, they are applicable and adaptable to everyone's life situation… they merit, I believe, attention and reflection.

1. We all have things in our lives that "disable" us, that cause us to feel we cannot attain or accomplish or achieve success. These things may be related to physical issues, matters of temperament, emotional predispositions, harsh upbringing, lack of resources, difficult environment, etc., etc. They may be visible to others or hidden within. What I learned was that it's easy to use these as excuses but more productive to use them as motivation. We can choose to succumb or to overcome.

2. The very things that we identify as adversities can provide us with a bountiful supply of immensely useful gifts. My difficulty in seeing out into this world helped me to develop a capacity for insights and internal reflection. The taunts about thick glasses encouraged me to have deeper empathy for others enduring unkindness. I found myself able to trust intuition and to envision/imagine what I could not see, abilities that became tools beneficial in establishing relationships and doing planning. It is essential that we open ourselves to the gifts presented to us by adversity.

3. Going through a difficult situation or through trying times can give us a whole new attitude and approach to life. This may seem an obvious point, but what is less obvious but absolutely crucial is our response to the questions…. Is our new attitude/approach based in bitterness or optimism? Does it bog us down or buoy us up? Is it discouraging or enabling? Does it cause us to hold a grudge or release us to discover new sources of energy? Is it dominantly negative or persuasively positive? Through my own experience of having to struggle from behind, I chose to become tenacious, to welcome challenges, to develop a solid work ethic. If we deal with trials and difficulties with a sense of gratitude for the opportunities they offer, we can respond to the questions I listed by making wise and uplifting choices.

4. There will be people in our lives who take personal risks for our sake, people who want us to be able to reach our potential, people who believe in us or recognize abilities we may not ourselves be aware of. It could be a teacher, a boss, a spouse or partner, a coach, a business colleague. In my case, it was a courageous doctor who dared a difficult surgery because he wanted me to thrive as a sighted person. I think that, in a way, impact-persons in our lives tend to be those who enable us to see things we are blind to, who expand our vision of ourselves and the world, who deepen our insights. We need, quite simply, to be open to and thankful for such persons when they grace our lives.

My sincere hope is that by sharing what I have so far dealt with – things I have come to see and to understand – you'll be encouraged to look at your own life experiences as a power source for personal growth. I'll end this introduction (and invite you to enjoy the rest of the book!) by stating my core understanding: What you can't do does not define you, and what you can do is always greater. This, in a phrase, is what I've learned, what I've put in practice, what I've trusted to achieve a satisfying measure of success. What I write in the chapters ahead is intended to help you write your own personal success story, for I believe wholeheartedly that **if I can do it, you can, too!**

# 1. "No Magic"

Magic is the art of producing an unexpected, amazing or startling result… a rabbit out of a hat, a selected card showing up in someone's pocket, a person surviving being sawed in half, a large object disappearing. As we witness these things, we find ourselves making a swift transition from wonder to curiosity. We think to ourselves, "How did that happen?" And many of us begin to muse, "Hey, could I do that?" We want to know how the tricks are done. The magician, of course, is not eager to pass along that information – the magicians' code discourages such sharing – because his or her livelihood depends on maintaining the illusion of possessing mysterious powers or esoteric knowledge. More on that shortly.

I would make a lousy magician. Once I experienced the satisfaction of mastering a new trick, I'd want to provide others all the how-to information so they could enjoy a similar sense of satisfaction and accomplishment. Over decades in the financial services industry, I have produced results that some might consider magical. A steadily expanding business. Growing sales. Professional recognition. But there was no magic involved, and for me the results were neither unexpected nor amazing nor startling. How they happened – and how you can make them happen – is what I intend to share in this book.

I promised in the first paragraph to get back to the notion of mysterious powers and esoteric knowledge. It's obvious that for there to be new magicians emerging onto the scene, some practitioners have to share/sell/explain the methods they use, the so-called "tricks of the trade." For those of us in the business of sales and service, the "tricks of the trade" are not tricks at all. The powers are not mysterious. The knowledge is not esoteric. But just as a magician must get informed about obtaining the right tools, mastering the proper techniques, and developing a commitment to practice, so must you to become successful in sales. Will your results be magic? No. Can they be stunning and satisfying. Yes.

I'd like to share with you an experience in my life that was both moving and revelatory. At my first Million Dollar Round Table meeting in Boston years ago, I was more than a bit awestruck at the caliber of the talent in attendance and quickly succumbed to the feeling that: "These people are different from me. They're better… smarter… more adept… more qualified." I was viewing them as magicians who could pull off dazzling sales tricks that I could never hope to do. One of the presenters at the meeting was Marv Feldman (a master magician in my eyes at the time!) who gave a superb, polished talk. Seated in the front row as he spoke was his father Ben (a legendary wizard in the industry!). At this point in his life, Ben was confined to a wheelchair. Following his son's talk, people crowded around Ben to greet him, to convey best wishes, to seek an autograph.

Later that day, while walking through a skywalk connecting hotels, I saw Marv with his mother and father. He was pushing Ben's wheelchair. I approached them, thanked Marv for his helpful talk and told Ben how much I admired his contributions to our industry. I shook his now-frail hand and in that moment, really a family moment, I was struck by our common humanity. I could see that Ben and I were not separated by some mystical, magical gulf. He and I were both persons granted the gift of life with all its pluses and perils, both blessed with talents to use and to develop. The difference was that he had used his to produce an income with more zeroes at the end of it! I am grateful for that meeting, for the grace of the Feldman family, for a crucial self-understanding. That moment of insight has motivated me ever since, for through it I became convinced that I could be as able as anyone once I stopped trying to find the magic and focused on tools, techniques and practice.

Marv helped me along with this new direction. At the Million Dollar Round Table meeting, Marv's talk had referenced an anonymous client and the management of a huge investment. Shortly after I returned home,

I received from Marv a one-page statement listing ways to minimize or eliminate estate taxes. This was the tool-kit he assembled to address his client's specific needs. Estate taxes do not go away by "magic;" they must be addressed using specific and specialized tools of the trade.

It occurred to me, as I used the information Marv had sent, that every client contact presented me with a work order – something that needed to be done – and that I would be wise to create a sheet listing needed tools (ideas, products, expertise, etc.). To identify which ones the work required. To make sure I knew how to use them. To set my priorities on order of use.

A friend of mine told me about a group of people in his community who are learning from a master carver how to create exquisite representations of birds. The tool kit required for coaxing life-like birds from an inert block of wood is a set of purpose-specific knives and chisels. And the instructor's first words to students were these: "Keep you tools sharp! If you don't, you'll butcher your project and probably hurt yourself." These words of advice can be applied verbatim to the context of business. What they mean in practical terms is staying informed and up-to-date about the tools-of-the-trade that you use in the daily practice of your work. Just as figures of birds do not emerge magically from chunks of wood, well-crafted responses to the needs of clients are not created by means of magic. In my own work, I must be familiar with contracts, investment portfolio options, binders, annuities, tax regulations, insurance products, and more. I have to stay sharp in my knowledge of these tools. Only then can I use them effectively and apply them with precision. Cutting edge tools and a keen mind… we need both.

The sheet Marv sent me did not provide any "how to use" directions, any instruction about technique. For that I am grateful. And you will note that this book neither promises nor provides you with a whiz-bang, never-fail system or method for making sales. That's magic, and as this chapter's title asserts, there is no magic to sales success.

Let's imagine that we have assembled a group of talented artists… and a squad of baseball players… and a gathering of violinists… and a bunch of chefs. We provide each group with appropriate tools-of-the-trade. Brushes and paints. Bats and balls. Instruments and bows. Skillets and knives. Then we place them in a setting where they can put these tools to use. It is an absolutely sure thing that the resulting performances and products within each group will vary widely. This is because every participant will apply techniques of use that are personal, techniques developed to best channel individual talents, preferences and skills.

The word "technique" comes from a Greek root meaning "art or craft." It is important to keep this in mind in our work. Selling is truly an art, not a mechanical task done by rote. It demands creativity, and that is where we need to pay serious attention to identifying and developing those individual techniques that enable us to achieve the greatest success.

This requires devoting yourself to a process of honest personal discernment. It means answering the question: What gifts/traits do I possess that allow me to access and apply tools/expertise/knowledge in ways that meet the needs of clients. Some of us have a gift of gab – of schmoozing – that establishes an immediate comfort level. Others have a deftness with numbers and organization. Some of us use humor to put folks at ease and draw out information. Others have an encyclopedic understanding of products. Some of us need time to assess and reflect. Others have brainbursts of immediate ideas. It is vital to know your own gifts and tendencies… these will shape a sales technique that is uniquely personal. Here is the crucial point: Each one of us must own what is our own. Or, in other words, we must be ourselves – fully and honestly – or we will come across as phony. And we know that phoniness is never the basis for ongoing success.

Having a well-stocked tool kit and finding a sales technique that is definitively your own are necessities… but they are useless unless put into practice. Doctors and lawyers refer to what they do as "having a practice" because with every patient/client contact they are putting in practice the skills and techniques they have acquired. And every athlete knows that success in a game, match or event is entirely dependent on focused and rigorous practice.

Practice in sales has much in common with the professions just noted. It differs radically from the practice-motives of a magician. Remember – no magic! The magician wants to hide what he or she is doing in order to produce a surprising result. In practicing our sales skills – using the tools and techniques we possess – our goal is to let clients know exactly what we are doing in order to produce a defined and, as much as possible, predictable result. Good physicians and attorneys keep those they are serving fully informed. Good sales persons do the same.

One more note -- an important one – on how the practice efforts of sales persons parallel those of athletes. A successful career for both means attaining the highest possible levels of achievement. So we need to practice as if our goal is the equivalent of reaching the Super Bowl, World Series, World Cup or Masters. This requires, in practical terms, devoting one day of every week to contacting and meeting with high-end prospects. Without fail. This takes personal discipline and commitment. It means strengthening your personal presentation by doing the sales-skill equivalent of an extra lap or an added set of push-ups. One day of every week, challenge yourself with the opportunity to achieve a significant professional win, and from each meeting with a high-end prospect, take away an understanding of what skills most need practice in order to enhance future performance…. We will be talking about identifying and interacting with prospects at other places in this book, too.

The message of this chapter is one intended to encourage you. There is no magic to sales. You do not need special incantations to cast a spell over clients. Through the years of my career, I have carefully assembled the tools of my trade (through professional development, self-study, reflection on my own experience, sharing ideas with other successful persons). I have found sales techniques that are genuine, open, comfortable, inviting and thoroughly "me." I have practiced my craft with the discipline of an athlete and have challenged myself to engage with high-end prospects every week. I have worked no magic but have worked hard at the process I share with you. It has brought success as well as tremendous personal satisfaction. And I know that **if I can do it, you can, too!**

# 2. "Valuing Humility"

I believe that in order to become the best sales person you can be you must become the best person you can be. If I did not believe that fervently, I would not have included this chapter on humility. My point is that personal qualities and character have a significant role in shaping sales success. I realize that in a business that rewards and gives accolades to those who achieve high levels of productivity, it may be strange to stress humility, but my goal is to provide you with advice that is more enduring than obvious.

If we look at admirable and notable persons over the course of history – world leaders, religious figures, premier achievers in the arts and in athletics, geniuses in literature and science, legends in our own industry – one trait that stands out, that emerges as something in common, is humility. This is striking and noteworthy. So let's look at why this is so.

It's often helpful to look at the roots of a word to understand the depth of its meaning. This is absolutely the case when we examine "humility." This word comes from an Old French word meaning, among other things, "in the ground." It further relates to the Latin word "humus," meaning earth, specifically the part of earth that is fertile and promoting of growth. So… if we look at the word origins and make a subtle extension, to be humble means, in a very real sense, to be "grounded." Grounded in a way that is fertile and productive.

Humility is an essential. Our industry thrives when it places the emphasis of effort on our clients. We excel, collectively and individually, when we replace interests that are self-satisfying, self-fulfilling, self-serving with those that are other-heeding, other-focused, other-serving.

I want to share with you two examples of how humility either defined or shaped a person. Einstein and me! When Albert Einstein came to the United States, he was the most valuable intellectual property on the planet. He agreed to come to Princeton, New Jersey, to be a resident scholar at The Institute for Advanced Study. When it came time for him to move from New York City to Princeton, a date was set and transportation arranged. Dr. Einstein would arrive by train at Princeton Junction. On the appointed day, town dignitaries, a band and a crowd of locals gathered to greet the great man. The train arrived… but no Dr. Einstein. Assuming he had missed the train, everyone waited for the next arrival. Again, no Dr. Einstein. Panic set in. Calls to New York City confirmed that he had left. Visions of kidnappers arose. The band left. The crowd left. Then, in downtown Princeton, someone discovered Dr. Einstein, who had somehow made his way to town from the train station undetected, doing what he most loved… sitting in a store eating ice cream. When asked how he got there, he said, somewhat sheepishly, "I'm sorry. I didn't think anyone would be waiting to greet me. There was a seat on an earlier train, so I took it." Then, back to his ice cream. The man who possessed perhaps the greatest scientific mind of the twentieth century also possessed great humility. If he could do it, we can, too!

And we should. Pride is a personal and business liability. A composite definition of pride taken from several sources is this: "having an unduly high or inordinate opinion of one's own knowledge, importance or merits… often revealed through overbearing attitudes or demeaning the worth of others' feelings or capabilities." It is a thoroughly off-putting trait and, whatever your religious dispositions, you can understand why medieval folks put it as the first of the "seven deadly sins." It does not draw positive response from others and in fact attracts quite the opposite. Don't we enjoy seeing a boastful, self-inflated person have his/her ego pricked? Don't we feel a degree of satisfaction when someone who has placed himself/herself on a pedestal takes a bit of a tumble?

It is so sensible to be humble… yet how seductive to succumb to pride. I confess that I did on one occasion early in my career. Example number two. The occasion was that of my first professional paid speaking engagement. Some time before I was scheduled to be on, one of the event-workers called me over to attach my wireless microphone. I made small talk and acted like the process was entirely familiar. In truth, I had never been miked before. I thanked him and wandered around chatting with friends and colleagues. I felt like a star. Just before speaking time, I made my way to a rest room and, as I began pushing open the door, I got a tap on the shoulder and a friendly piece of advice: "You might not want to go in there with a hot mike." It was an immensely timely lesson in on-off switch technology… and a welcome ego-puncturing, tumble-from-the-pedestal moment. If we are fortunate, we will have friends or family or circumstances that gently teach us the importance of humility. It is, however, up to us to listen and to take the lessons to heart.

So what does all this have to do with excelling as someone engaged in sales? Doesn't it take a certain amount of drive and confidence to achieve success? Absolutely. But my point is this: humility neither contradicts nor diminishes drive and confidence. Rather, humility complements and amplifies them by helping you become the best person you can be.

There are a half-dozen significant ways that humility has a profoundly positive impact on your sales contacts with others, on your place in the community/business, on your personal growth and on your career as a whole.

1. Humility reveals to clients your genuine "not-about-me" self. This assumes, of course, that you have nurtured and developed that self. A good way to check that out is to monitor your McLandress Coefficient. My what?! This measurement was developed by a quirky but brilliant Harvard psychology professor as a way to quantify a person's level of self-absorption. Simply put, it is the longest span of time a person can go in conversation or written materials without using "I," "me" or "my." (You can even check online for ratings of past historical figures!) Being meaningfully engaged with a client certainly requires using personal pronouns, but the point of bringing up the McLandress Coefficient is this: "you" and "your" should be the dominant ones.

You may be highly accomplished and competent, but it is a caring attitude and satisfying, goal-centered results that truly convey these things. You may have garnered some prestigious awards or accolades but, to be honest, these are transitory adornments. What clients care about is who you are consistently as someone devoted to their best interests.

A friend of mine who is in sales has a favorite phrase she reminds herself of each day: "If you are completely full of yourself, you have no room for others." Perhaps these words should be on a sign in all our offices.

2. Humility enables you to affirm that your relationship with clients is a partnership. This is an extension of my first point about putting forth a "not-about-me" self. This begins with a couple humble recognitions: not a single one of us knows everything or never makes a mistake. It is vitally important that you do not present yourself as all-knowing about products or strategies or, perhaps worse, as "knowing best" all answers to a client's stated needs. Such a presentation comes across as pretentious, foolish or arrogant. Probably all three! In a relationship that is truly a partnership there is a deep mutual respect. I find it crucial to note whenever appropriate and possible: "You're right about that." "Your idea is better." "You know your needs best and we'll work together to realize them." It is also essential, when circumstances call for it, to be able/willing to say, "I was wrong." This is not a sign of weakness, not an admission of incompetence. It is, rather, what an honest partner says to another. And it conveys something of ongoing importance to clients… that you are forthright, that you are using your critical thinking abilities to review and reassess their situation, that you will work with them on new ideas to meet their needs.

3. Humility is attractive. In a culture that seems to produce an abundance of posers, pretenders and self-promoters, a person who is capable and humble will stand out. Two characteristics of genuinely humble persons: They do not "blow their own horn" at personal achievements; they know that consistent attention to clients speaks loudly. And, they appreciate that the most effective advertising they will ever get is when others speak well of their work; accolades and affirmations from others are way better than anything self-generated.

Since being humble is pretty much the opposite of being flashy and attention-seeking, what makes it attractive to clients? Quite simply, a sales person who is able, stable and humble attracts clients because they recognize/sense that he/she will be focused attentively on them, on their hopes and goals and needs. Someone who comes across as diverted by personal self-interests is, and should be, decidedly unattractive.

Most of us pay attention to our appearance when we are in a business context… we strive to be well-groomed and well-dressed. But what we wear on the inside is even more important, and I advocate putting on humility. You can choose to put it on or you can set it aside, much as you can do with an article of clothing. But I guarantee that if you choose to become humble, you will find that the choice becomes you. You will become a better and more attractive individual… a better an more attractive sales person.

4.  Humility generates generosity. Through the years, I've found that the greater my success in business, the more I recognize and reflect upon the fact that I have benefited from the support of friends and family and colleagues, the wisdom shared with me by others, the circumstances that have provided me with opportunities. My success, I see, is a combination of what I have worked to achieve and what other persons and life conditions have enabled. Net insight… success is not about me, and my wisest response is to adopt the role of grateful beneficiary.

This is a perspective grounded in humble gratitude, and it is an energizing one! It urges me to look around to see how I can reach out to enrich the lives of others in my family, my community, my industry, my world. Let me explain. Take the self-absorbed view of life: It asserts that, "I'm the most important, so I'll keep everything for myself." Time, talents and financial assets are all viewed as possessions rather than as potential gifts to benefit others.

Those who seek our services are generally motivated by wanting to have a degree of personal security, but also by a desire to benefit others – loved ones, institutions, larger causes. To humbly model generosity is something that will be personally fulfilling as well as something that will be noted by clients. All of us can find, as I have for decades, places where our skills can make a real difference, where our targeted funds can help create a better world, where our commitment of time can touch and change lives. And as a postscript, I want to add that in our industry – through volunteering as a speaker or teaching a course in an area of expertise – there are always opportunities to give back.

Remember… a humble person, motivated by gratitude and inclined to self-giving, does not act in order to gain admiration, but he or she, for that very reason, is often very much admired.

5. Humility forges a discipline that trains us to examine how our actions affect – in a primary way – the well-being of others. A prideful, self-important person approaches life with questions such as: How can I get the best or get what I want out of this relational transaction? How can I manipulate or dominate this person? How can I use this situation to come out looking best? These questions are deadly entry points for someone involved in sales. More humble and appropriate ones are: How can we build a relationship that is mutually beneficial? How can we work together most effectively? How can we best use this situation to develop a mutual respect? There are certain internal statements or assumptions that have their base in an undefined pride. Things such as: I have the answers. I know what's best. I think you need to do this. I want this thing to happen. I'm sure of it…. To move toward that second set of questions and away from those self-centered statements requires both a willingness to do some serious self-assessment and a capacity for personal change.

6. Humility roots us in where we came from. No matter how successful we are in our business, every single one of us had to build that success from the ground up. It is good to remind ourselves of humble beginnings when we knew nothing, had no income and no clients. That recollection of where we once were helps us to appreciate where we now are and to reaffirm what it will take to achieve more… energy, planning, focus, hard work, giving of ourselves.

I share with you now an example of someone whose actions and approach to life demonstrate the power and scope of humility. She is a highly successful executive and an avid competitive runner. Her reason for running, aside from the health benefits, is one she put this way: "It keeps me humble. I began by just walking fast, then jogging, then moving on to serious training. I've always been intent on getting better, and I have, but there will always be someone faster than I am. That gives me a real balance between appreciating my accomplishments and admiring someone else's." She recounted a time of being a few miles into a training run and feeling exceptionally pleased. At that moment, without even hearing the light footfalls behind her, she got briskly passed by a woman who was probably into her tenth mile or more of a run; it was a former winner of the Olympic marathon who used the same course of roads. It was time for a self-effacing smile. This person also pursues a peculiar hobby as she runs. Erratically, every now and then, she will stop to pick up something from the pavement. When asked about this, she laughed and said: "It's quirky-looking, I know. A friend told me that at my level of income I should be embarrassed to be seen picking up coins. Frankly, that wouldn't embarrass me at all. My image is far less important to me than my intentions. What I'm actually doing is picking up nails or screws or sharp pieces of metal… anything that could puncture a tire. I remember when I was a young mother and just starting out in business. A flat tire was a major blow… the cost of replacement, the missed appointment, the waste of time, the hassle for my child, the sense of vulnerability. So – if I can save someone from those concerns, I'm truly happy to do that. It's a tiny action, a minor interruption in my training. I've picked up hundreds of nails over the decades!"

What a great example of humility and of its impact…. Remembering one's origins. Developing consistent habits of generous spirit that benefit persons beyond one's self. Being willing to acknowledge the achievements of others. Having an humility-grounded confidence that values doing good over looking good.

In our business, reaching the Top of the Table is a notable achievement. And it can test us if we allow it to let us lapse into feelings of self-importance. I've felt that temptation. But I have also learned what I pass along: If you meet with success, it is crucial to remain the person you are, the person who attained it. You can be grateful for gaining what is prestigious without becoming pretentious.

Humility is an attribute that has no downside. Striving for it is a conscious choice. And if you put in the time and effort toward developing it, there is abundant return on investment. Take on the challenge. I'm confidant that **if I can do it, you can, too.**

# 3. "Listening"

"Listen to what I'm telling you." Parents speak those words to children when instructing or correcting them. "Listen up!" Coaches and officers and other group leaders use this command to gain attention before conveying expectations or delivering orders. "Listen carefully." Doctors and counselors and spiritual leaders and many other professionals say this as a preface to laying out key insights or explaining a set of options. And though most of us in our business do not explicitly state to clients, "Listen to all the information I'm giving you," we do have that expectation.

But.... are we being good, intent, caring, focused listeners ourselves? That is a question we need to be able to meet with a strong positive response. In this chapter, I'll provide you with some materials to reflect upon and some suggestions to implement, both in service to helping you be able to say as a personal affirmation, "I'm committed to being a good listener."

Several years ago at a prestigious small private college, a freshman got called into the office of the dean of admissions. She was apprehensive, but the dean smiled and extended his hand. "I just wanted to meet you. You're going to be a very busy young woman. In the freshman class this year over four hundred people said on their admission forms that they were great leaders. You're the only one who stated that you were an excellent follower. Congratulations on knowing your strength." Truly excellent listeners are about as rare as that particular college freshman. Yet, as with her, it can be a strength.

In the introduction to this book, I recounted the story of my severe eye problems in childhood. This presented me with plenty of challenges but also provided a tremendous opportunity. Since I did not have access to the visual cues that convey much meaning in conversation, I had to be especially sensitive to what my ears took in… the words, the inflections of voice, the ways things were phrased, the tones, the timings. I learned early on the difference between listening and hearing. Hearing is a sense. Listening is a skill.

The simple fact is that you can hear without listening. So when someone claims, "You haven't heard a word I said," his or her true annoyance is not that you are deaf to auditory stimuli… it's that you seem disengaged from or uninterested in the message being conveyed. More precisely, the complaint is: "You took in my sounds but paid no attention to my meaning!" All of us notice when someone to whom we are speaking seems to be "somewhere else," to have wandering attention, to be mentally engaged in preparing something to say. Most of us would choose to avoid people who displayed this kind of off-putting behavior. That is certainly the case with clients. So it's worth reminding ourselves often that our clients don't ask to be listened to… they expect it. And rightly so. Bottom line, our value to a client begins with our ability to listen… to needs, hopes, requirements, dreams, goals. Paradoxically, some of these things may be unstated in the actual words we hear, but we will be able to discern and identify them if we are adept listeners.

As I noted earlier, hearing is a sense and listening is a skill. This is good news, for though senses can be enhanced, a skill can be learned. What I'll be offering you are some broad suggestions that can help you learn to become a listener, a better listener, an excellent listener. I'll also share how I emphasize listening in the context of client contacts. Practical applications:

- Make the commitment to value the skill of listening. As identified, my eye issues predisposed me to focus on listening. But visual impediments aside, the conversations at our dinner table featured my father's oft-stated remarks about the greatest leaders being the best listeners and his constant reference to the fact that "we were created with two ears and one mouth." Such an upbringing had its influence on me, but it was my eighth grade teacher's stress on life-long learning that made me do something I urge for you….

- Develop your skills of listening and observation through exercises designed to strengthen them. My teacher had us write down everything we remembered hearing and seeing on the way to school. My classmates and I at first thought this to be a pretty stupid exercise, and our lists were handed in quite rapidly with sparse details. But the more we did it, the longer our assignments became and the more we found ourselves learning about the world around us. This was not a stupid exercise at all, and it's one I commend to you. Use it in whatever form and format suits you. For us, it turned an entire class of teenagers into more attentive observers and betters listeners. That said….

- We need to be willing and able to target our listening to specific circumstances. I'll get back to this when addressing the way we listen to clients, but for now I'll simply illustrate how listening skills are context (and habit!) specific. A friend of mine brought a group of fifth and sixth graders from New York City up into the wilderness mountains of Maine. On their first hike, they talked loudly and listened to various electronic devices, behaviors my friend allowed. When he brought them to a stopping place at a granite overlook, he said, "For the next minute, I want no talking at all and all electronics turned off." There was grumbling compliance. At the end of a minute, he asked, "What did you hear?" And the kids all agreed, "Nuthin'!" Compared to the din of their home environment, this mountainside was, for them, stone silent. "OK," my friend said, "Let me tell you a few things you might try listening for." He mimicked the sound of several birds he knew were in the area, told them that squirrels and chipmunks rustled things on the ground and in the trees, commented on the whir that the wind gusts made now and then, described a couple insect sounds, noted that the distant cars could be heard occasionally from a far-off road, even told them to listen to their own breathing and small movements. Over the next couple minutes, eyes widened; the children practiced a new skill and so could listen to what an unfamiliar environment had to tell them. This is a dramatic example, but it illustrates how we need to develop listening skills that allow us to attune ourselves to a particular setting… or circumstance… or client. The example also serves as a reminder that: creating an inner personal quietness allows us to become listeners in any situation. In relation to conversations with clients, this amounts to being an exercise in and commitment to selflessness. To client-centeredness (cf. the preceding chapter). Since this is the very essence of what we say we are about in our business, it merits some more detailed discussion.

In my experience, there are three specific things that routinely impair our ability to attain the personal quietness that enables us truly to listen to our clients. I offer them to you not merely to identify them. That's helpful, but unless you monitor your own tendencies and behaviors with the intent of eliminating these impediments to listening, my identification is just useless (non-utilized) knowledge. So as we look at them, I encourage you to begin thinking about how you can avoid or set aside these things that can block hearing what you need to hear.

1. If we pay more attention to thinking about what we're going to say than to what the client is telling us, our attention is clearly divided and incomplete. Pre-planning our own potential output gets in the way of hearing a client's presented input. It is easy to succumb to the temptation of formulating a response that seems clever or insightful or astute or even brilliant. But that temptation is in fact grounded in something inherently selfish – the desire to look good. Better, far better, to take in all information carefully before attempting to work on what we will say, on what we offer as advice. If we say anything while listening to a client, it is usually best if it is in the form of clarifying questions that do not impede the client's flow of thought but indicate that we are intently gathering/processing information.

2. If we carry into conversation with a client the things that are concerns, issues and agenda items in our personal lives, we will definitely be impaired listeners. We will be guilty of "listening under the influence" of such internal questions as: "Am I going to make it to my daughter's soccer game?… Did that person I met at the party really like me?… Is

my spouse still mad at what I said last night?... Did I pay that bill or is the bank statement wrong?... Is my mother needing some home care?... Am I going to get along with that new co-worker?... Are my workouts getting the result I want?" These are the kinds of things that occupy our thoughts on a regular basis. But, to be honest, they cannot be allowed to intrude into our interaction with a client.

Some years ago, the Eagles released a song titled, "Take It Easy." And a line from the lyrics is pertinent. It says, "Don't let the sound of your own wheels drive you crazy." The wheels that spin subconsciously in our minds, the wheels that revolve around our personal "stuff," can create a noise that deafens us to the voiced concerns of our clients. We need to find ways to silence this clutter and clatter. Awareness of this interior noise is the crucial first step.

3.  If we pre-determine what products we want to offer a client, we will listen selectively and not entirely. Earlier, I noted that we need to have the capacity to target our listening to specific circumstances. In the broadest possible sense, every client brings to us a set of unique, personally specific circumstances. When we listen as a client describes them, we can formulate a plan to provide for needs and to meet goals. But when we are programmed to provide only certain products or solutions, when we are on a "track" that takes a client where we want him or her to go, we are not genuinely listening at all. We become insensitive to our client's specific circumstances because we are sidetracked in the direction of meeting our own needs and goals.

We all know that a one-track mind is not an open mind, not a mind capable of listening. But there's good news. We can address this situation in a forthright manner by developing a deep knowledge of a variety of products, by committing ourselves to thinking creatively about their application to specific circumstances. This takes some hard work over time to be sure (there's a chapter on that later in this book!), but it will enable us to listen with absolute openness.

I approach every contact with a client as an exercise in listening. When I meet a new client, I typically say, "Tell me about yourself and your upbringing." Then I sit back and listen, perhaps offering brief questions or making short comments that encourage more self-disclosure. When I sense an appropriate time, I ask, "What are you here for?" At this point, I do not reach for a pen to make notes…. I purely listen. This is a time when I gain important insights and information, and I have communicated that the person speaking to me is my priority. Only if a client says something to the effect of, "I came to hear what you have to say," do I begin to lay out a process for going forward. And only when a client describes and identifies needs/goals/hopes do I name specific products as options.

Given that establishing a relaxed question-and-answer format seems the best way to evolve towards meeting those needs/goals/hopes, I have some rules I try hard to follow; they work for me!

- Never ask a question you really don't want an answer to. (There's wisdom to conciseness and restraint!)

- Never anticipate an answer. (Be open to surprises!)

- Never answer for someone. (Have respect!)

- Never provide a single set answer. (Keep options alive!)

Listening – as a skill and as an art and as a discipline – has so much to commend it that it merits a full chapter in this book. Listening is, in our business, an essential tool to building success. When we listen to persons, it conveys the clear message that we value them. And when we remember the needs/goals/hopes they express, it conveys that we care for them and about them. Professionally, our listening demands remembering. This is key. Clients rightly expect us to remember what they say. Baseline, having to repeat what they have previously stated is annoying to clients. And it should be.

I have been blessed with an excellent memory. Not everyone has such a gift. If remembering things is a challenge, it is worth spending the time and resources to amplify and sharpen your memory capacity. Through courses, readings and exercises, you can expand your abilities. It's not only crucial to your success… it's also fun! If you need any nudging toward increasing memory capacity, consider this: remembering makes a consistently positive impact. If you remember the essentials or the details of a client's life, it will be recognized and appreciated. Remembrance conveys compassion and concern. Clients notice. Creating reliable and accessible memory aids is invaluable. In whatever form you choose, keep accurate records that help you recognize and recall key dates, family members, issues, concerns, significant life-shaping events, hobbies, quirky likes and dislikes, serious fears, etc.

There's a story I love about two psychiatrists who shared an office building. Each day they would go up an elevator to start their day and descend the elevator at day's end. Without fail, one of the psychiatrists would enter the elevator at the end of a day with haggard expression, disheveled clothes, glazed eyes and droopy posture. The other would enter with snappy attire, cheerful demeanor and bright eyes. After months of noting this, the beleaguered psychiatrist asked his counterpart, "How do you listen to the anguished, tormented tales of your patients and still come out as you do?" His colleague answered, "So who listens?" … The point this story makes is that of noting and affirming that listening is not easy. It takes effort, practice, intent, patience. But here's a guarantee: the more you develop your capacity to listen, the more you will stand out.

One final point. In a world abounding with an overwhelming amount of input, it is necessary to determine what we truly need to listen to and what we can legitimately, carefully tune out. This means creating a kind of filter that helps us achieve the personal quietness I spoke of earlier. This filter is a very individual thing. What some consider essential to hear in unimportant to others. Noise to some is music to others…. For me, I begin with making sure that my personal quietness always keeps me receptive to the voices of family and friends, the ever-changing needs of clients and community, the trends of the market and our broader culture, the beckonings of health maintenance and recreation. I realize, of course, that the notion of a filter is a concept – nothing can precisely regulate what we take in from the world, but it is essential, in a complex world, to guard against the input overload that can stress, distress and wear us down. So it is certainly worth taking the time and investing the reflective energy in assessing what, of all we hear, we need truly to listen to and to allow inside our space of personal quietness.

It may seem a daunting task to shape oneself into being an excellent listener. That said, it is crucial to remember what I stated early on in this chapter: listening is a skill, and as such it can be learned and strengthened. I did not begin my career as a superb listener, but I practiced and improved and noticed this: greater proficiency as a listener propelled my business success and enriched my personal life. I wish the same for you. I encourage your steadfast commitment to becoming the best listener you can be, and I'm confident that **if I can do it, you can, too!**

# 4. "Hard Work"

A friend of mine who has achieved success through application of a resoundingly strong work ethic once told me, "One thing I regret never thanking my parents for was giving me household chores to do from toddler-age up." When I press for a bit more explanation, he said this: "Mom and Dad explained that families need every member to help with all the 'what needs to get done' stuff. My father explained logically, 'If we all do our tasks, there'll be more time for fun.' So by age three I was handing my mother the clothes from a basket for her to iron. At age five it was carrying dishes to the sink and pulling weeds. By seven I'd moved on to emptying trash, scrubbing bathroom tile, dusting and washing windows. Mind you, none of this was connected with my small allowance which was considered a weekly gift – one that could be revoked for bad behavior. When I got to be ten, the chores continued, but I was introduced to the concept of earned income. I got paid for mowing the lawn, washing the car, shoveling snow and such. Of this money, I could spend half and I had to save half." When I asked what this childhood regimen taught, he stated: "It was, pure and simple, character development. I learned that hard work has rewards. And I've come to realize that businesses are in many ways similar to family households in terms of task-sharing." He paused and said, "My two children who grew up with chores are now in supervisory roles in healthcare and academic settings. They say the biggest personnel issue is dealing with those who take it as a personal affront to be asked to put in defined and necessary hard work."

To become successful, you cannot allow those personnel problems to be as a personal problem in terms of your willingness to put in goal-specific hard work. My friend was right in observing that hard work is a crucial component of childhood character development. And though he didn't extend that understanding to professional character development in later years, I want to affirm that it is absolutely the case. While hard work does not guarantee business success, it vastly increases the probability, and ignoring it pretty much puts the possibility of success in the dumpster. Clearly no one, looking back over a career, wants to be in the position of admitting, "You know, I really didn't put in the effort."

Reviewing my own job history, it occurred to me that my early work years taught me some seriously significant values. I can't say I identified them all clearly at the time (I sort of absorbed them and made them part of who I am), but I recognize now tremendous benefits of regularly identifying and assessing the values we derive from the hard work we do. If we are to become value-able persons – those who act from a sturdy principled core – such assessment is vital.

For my first job I had a paper route. For a boss I had me. For a sales/ customer-acquisition person I had me. For an accountant I had me. For a collection department I had me. For product delivery I had my throwing arm. For transportation equipment I had feet or a bike. This one-child-buy-for-wholesale-sell-at-retail operation, in which I was responsible for everything, taught me plenty. It taught me to value warm clothes on frigid Wisconsin mornings, for sure. But it also taught me values I carry with me every day: a dedication to <u>self-discipline</u> and a capacity for <u>multi-tasking</u>.

My second job as a mid-teen featured an unforgettable level of monotony. It involved picking sticks out of newly tilled land. All day long. Days upon days upon weeks upon weeks. This was brutally hot work as well. My diligence and persistence eventually led to the reward of driving some trucks. I cannot say I enjoyed this phase of my employment history, but again, I learned some crucial values: developing an ability to make it through <u>tedious work</u> and counting on <u>perseverance</u> as a means to achieving a better position.

My next job as an older teen was picking peas. This segued into driving a combine all day long. Since crops don't linger in an ideal state of ripeness for an extended period, harvest means urgent effort and long hours. The rhythm of labor was six weeks of this: up at the crack of dawn, drive all day into evening, ride home, catch a bite to eat and a nap, repeat day after day. I learned what sleep deprivation felt like and how I could remain functional while in a state of semi-exhaustion. Not ideal, but informative. In addition, since I had absolutely no time to spend any money, I discovered myself with a surprising accumulation of funds when my job ended. I was sort of the beneficiary of a thrift imposed by circumstance. This phase of my employment history – again noteworthy for its lack of glamor! – taught me to value these things: the strength developed through endurance and the amazing way that savings can grow.

When I got my first position in an actual office setting, the environment was almost too comfortable... air conditioning and heat were unaccustomed luxuries. And sitting at a desk making calls seemed like retirement. Fortunately, I recognized early on that my ethic of hard work had to get transferred and even amplified in this new situation. I reminded myself daily of a simple fact: laziness is not conducive to productivity. That's a statement worth typing into your laptop or fashioning into a sign for your desktop.

Self-discipline and multi-tasking -- A basic building block of business success is that of finding what you do better than anyone else. This will take some trial and error, and it demands absolutely honest, accurate self-assessment. Back when Walt Disney began his pioneering work in animation, he learned about every aspect of the process: story-writing, cartooning, financing, running projectors and sound equipment, choosing sites and materials, selling concepts and products, etc. But he also surrounded himself with people whose talent could be relied up to let him do what he did best – creative thinking and marketing. Though always capable as a multi-tasker, Disney exercised an honest self-discipline that prompted him to make the wise decision to focus his energy on what he did best. The results of that decision are one of the most stunning successes in business history.

It does truly take self-discipline to refrain from attempting to "do everything." "I can do it all," may make us feel important and busy, but adhering to that belief is exhausting, delusional and foolish. Sane, productive multi-tasking means that we only exercise that skill on the activities at which we are most able. We all need that firm self-discipline and discernment to define what we do better and more effectively than others, and to hire persons with complementary skills for other tasks. This we can label <u>directed</u> hard work. Mr. Disney is a pretty good model to follow.

Tedious work and perseverance -- Sure, we'd all like a job filled with exciting new concepts, creative challenges, brilliantly innovative products, engaging personal interactions. The good news in our industry is that at times we'll get a taste of all these things. But not every day. Many days will contain tasks that seem repetitive and just about as tedious as pulling sticks out of a freshly tilled field. One of these tasks, familiar to all of us, is keeping up contact with clients and prospects. It's always tempting to avoid or put off calls; rigorously holding to a schedule can seem taxing and tedious. This is, however, necessary hard work. Just as a field must be readied for planting to lead to a successful harvest, so it is with clients and prospects. We need to be preparing the field so it will be receptive to what we sow. This is tedious work.

It also does not always lead to a bountiful harvest. I absolutely realize that many of these calls feel like failures… So… I need to say a few words on failure! Thomas Edison, legendary innovator and inventor, tried hundreds of materials as possible filaments for an electric light bulb. He experienced hundreds of failures as he went through tedious repetitions of the testing process. As he discovered what didn't work in his painstaking exercises, he gained new insights into what might make the light come on and stay on. He practiced what we can term a <u>perceptive perseverance</u>. This is the kind we need to develop with a pattern of steadfast hard work. It is this that turns dull tedium into bright success.

Endurance and savings -- My early job experiences trained me for a work pattern I commend to all – get to work early, keep a discipline of hours, identify the purpose of what you do, push yourself enough to know your limits of effectiveness. In a nutshell, work hard! (Remember the benefits of what we've called "Chores!") This does not mean, as I'll note in another chapter on achieving balance in life, lapsing into the destructive patterns of workaholism. It does mean putting in all the energy/skill/effort you can. Simply showing up and accumulating hours is not enough. There's a wonderful story about a fellow who decided to make a job change after almost twenty years with one company. When his supervisor, listed as a reference, was asked by the potential new employer, "How long did Owen work for you?" he replied, "About thirty-six hours." The questioner was shocked and queried, "But he said he was employed with you for nearly two decades." "That is correct," said the supervisor, "And in that time he worked approximately thirty-six hours." This is not the kind of lackluster recommendation any of us would seek. And the clear message of that story is one to take to heart: presence must correspond to productivity.

What I have learned about the work activity of business is that it correlates to the physical activity of athletics. The more you put in hard work, the less arduous it feels. What seems difficult and clumsy at first becomes easier and more graceful. You develop a certain rhythm and inner sense of capability/capacity. Just as baseball pitchers and football quarterbacks and basketball shooting guards (and countless other athletes) develop, through painstaking drills that test their endurance, a feel for the "mechanics" of their task, so we can gain that sense of, "Yes, this is what I must do to be successful." In the case of athletes or desk-dwellers, the kind of hard work that tests the limits of endurance produces results. Strikeouts. Touchdowns. Three-point shots. Client contacts that assure income and afford the opportunity to acquire a satisfying, surprising amount of savings.

If you agree with what you've just read, you can choose to accept its urgings as a challenge. I encourage all my readers to review your personal history, to identify those times you recall as "hard work" and to evaluate honestly whether or not you are applying and adhering to the values you've discovered. (Perhaps they're similar to mine... self-discipline and risk-taking, tedious work and perseverance, endurance and saving). As you put in hard work in the future, constantly assess what you are learning. Don't ignore or set aside the obvious, and maintain an openness to subtle insights. Hard work always teaches a lesson.

Recognizing the value(s) and resolving to claim the benefits of hard work... **If I can do it, you can, too!**

# 5. "Gut Instinct"

In two previous chapters, we identified a specific personal quality to value and claim, and we described a particular skill to develop and practice. Humility – key to establishing enduring business relationships. Listening – essential to providing service that is client-based. In this chapter we will be looking at something that is a bit more raw: gut instinct. I am commending it to you not in its absolutely raw form that seems in conflict with true humility (which values the basic feelings and insights of others) and disdainful of careful listening (which hears the expressed desires and concerns of others). Gut instinct, in its refined and useful form, is the capacity to listen with humble gratitude – and a bit of wonder! – to the guiding wisdom of our inner sensitivities. Put another way, it means trusting a kind of visceral knowledge.

In terms of identifying both physical and emotional issues that need to be addressed, we probably all recognize that there is a good bit of wisdom in that folksy phrase: "The body don't lie." In fact, we are discovering more and more about what this "amazing machine" – our body – can tell us if we tune in and make the effort to listen. A bit more on some pertinent research findings later in the chapter.

If I am to have any credibility in my assertion that gut instinct is something to heed, develop and respect, I should put before you some examples from my own experience. I'll share four, all related to my business career.

1. As I have said earlier, my first job was that of delivering newspapers. Over time, my route grew and I had to deal with all the issues of a service-based business. One of these was non-payment or late payment. It became important for me to discern between those who

merited an extension of credit and those who did not. I should underscore the fact that non-payment meant money directly from my pocket since I had to purchase every paper delivered, so wise judgment was imperative. This discernment process provided me with the first time I learned to "trust my gut," and I discovered that these early business decisions were exceedingly accurate.

2. When I entered as a young man into the financial services business, a rational assessment of my experience and prospects would have led me to seek a job as an agent with an established firm. My gut instinct told me that though this appealed to the risk-averse side of me, it would not be where I would thrive or find contentment. So I started in business for myself. My basement office décor was Spartan-sparse… a desk and a chair, a phone, a box as file cabinet. It felt risky but right. Six months into my career, a banker told me that investing more into it would be a mistake. This is when I learned to trust my intuition. I borrowed against a credit card to hire a secretary and then moved to a client-welcoming office space. I now own the building in which I work. Gut instinct, which embodies a kind of inherent self-knowledge and self-understanding, guided me well.

3. Occasionally there will be micro-moments when you will be called upon to trust your gut instincts… or not. Pay attention to these decision points. Early in my career I made contact with someone who requested an appointment. His inquiries suggested a potentially lucrative connection. I made the appointment and drove to his impressive home. As I approached, I recalled my uneasiness at hearing the tone of his voice when confirming our meeting. Something had unsettled me, and so I drove on, the first appointment I had ever "blown off." Oddly, I felt totally at peace with this. And I never got a call questioning my non-appearance. Within months, this potential client was in the headlines for serious financial misdeeds. Instinct/intuition proved a lifesaver.

4. In 2006, I read a fair amount about a trending willingness people displayed for "throwing money at things": luxury goods, dubious financial products, real estate, high-flying stocks, hot technology items and such. The economy seemed to be chugging along nicely and many were encouraging folks either to acquire the unnecessary or to take a variety of investment risks. I was in Las Vegas for a speaking engagement and had just finished reading a related article. I looked out the window of my room at the development all over the place… or should I say, the over-development that was in place. It was something of a gut-punch, a warning that all was not well. Without hesitation, I began to exercise a more conservative and cautious approach in investments for myself and for clients. Within a couple years, that instinct-induced insight had proved its worth.

My inclination to follow gut instinct has served me well over time. Though such a course is not infallible, it has increased my comfort level in many decisions, and the track record cannot be ignored. A while back, a business coach with whom I was working helped confirm what I had come to trust through practice and experience. He told me that most successful entrepreneurs are intuitive/gut followers more than they are analyzers. They strike a balance of due diligence and following the guidance of instinct.

We make many of the most momentous choices in our lives without resorting to a rational decision-making process. In many instances, we "follow our heart." We select a life-partner on the basis of feelings that are often anything but rational, yet somehow we make a commitment in reliance on that inner sense of wanting to be with a specific person long-term. We choose friends and maintain friendships because of a sensed connection and not as the result of a data-driven assessment. We search for a dwelling place with certain criteria in mind, but we seldom buy or rent a place unless it <u>feels</u> like a place we can call home. We get all sorts of advice and input on dealing with issues that come up when raising children, but what most guides interactions with a child is something commonly referred to as "parental instincts." And if we ever get involved with managing or coaching an athletic team, even in an era of advanced analytics, we may experience positive results from "playing a hunch."

Our language abounds with phrases that suggest, in a variety of ways, how much we are informed by what might be called "the voices of our viscera." We speak of "not having the stomach" for a certain course of action, of bothersome items as things that "stick in my craw," of being "sick to my stomach" over something disturbing or unsettling. We enjoy a good "belly laugh" when we hear something humorous and refer to anguishing decisions as "gut-wrenching." Something that has a harsh impact?… a "gut punch." Something that demands the most from our emotional resources?… a "gut check." And, of course, all of us aspire to "have guts" when it comes to situations that test our principles or demand our courage.

Apart from the evidence provided by personal experience, it turns out that there seems to be good scientific backing supporting the practice of "going with the gut." Here is where we touch briefly on the research I alluded to earlier in this chapter. Harvard Medical School has confirmed a solid connection between our feelings and symptoms in our gut, and studies have shown the clear relationship between the gastrointestinal (GI) system and the brain. Our enteric nervous system (ENS), composed of over a hundred million nerve cells, is contained within our gastrointestinal tract and has been referred to by some scientists as our "second brain." Research at the Johns Hopkins Center for Neurogastroenterology has indicated that though this gut-based entity is not capable of thought, it does communicate with our big brain in ways we are continuing to discover…. All of this gives new depth to the significance of a gut instinct or intuition that truly emerges from our innards.

Note that I am not implying that gut instinct is infallible or that it should replace careful thought processes. But I am suggesting that there is something primal and honest about it that should be heeded and incorporated as a tool of the trade. That said, I want to share with you three things I have identified as hindrances to using gut instinct in a fully constructive manner. We need, I believe, to monitor and modify these tendencies in service to creating a kind of balanced approach that enables us to provide the best possible advice to clients. Here is the trio to watch out for....

First -- over-accumulating advice. All of us naturally seek out the wisdom or expertise of others. A humble, honest acknowledgement of our own limitations makes this a smart business practice. Over the course of time, we develop a cadre of writers/mentors/colleagues/researchers/industry experts upon whom we rely for accurate and pertinent information. The problem arises when we take in way too much advice. We become like someone who has gone to a smorgasbord, sampled everything available, and then finds it virtually impossible to move. Overindulging in advice can render us immobile in the area of decision-making. One can almost always find an opinion or piece of advice that contradicts or conflicts with what we have just taken in. The key is to be selective and limited. From the smorgasbord of advice that is available, develop the habit of selecting what you are quite certain to be delicious, nutritious, well-presented and satisfying. Yes, try new things, but have a discriminating appetite. Follow the best of your gut instincts.

Second -- allowing business clutter. We have probably all had instances in our lives of rummaging around in a drawer, closet, purse or toolbox as we search for a specific item. We say to ourselves, "I know it's here somewhere," as we waste minutes or more. In our business – or almost any client-centered service – there are countless things that need to be attended to, kept track of or sorted out. These are essentials, but they are in fact the minutiae of our work. Dealing with them can be as frustrating and time-consuming as that object search I just described. What is more impactful, though, is that these things impair our ability to follow our gut instincts. They distract us. They tie us up. We find ourselves paying more attention to the itty-bitties than to the nitty-gritties!

Instinct and intuition will not thrive unless they have plenty of room to get exercised. This means, quite simply, creating a business/office environment in which you do not trip over the minutiae. Technology can be useful in establishing such an environment. Setting up clear work processes is a help. But the crucial component is having capable, competent staff. I never regretted borrowing funds to hire my first office staff; I view all hirings as investments in enabling me to have the freedom to follow by best instincts. (More on investing in staff later in the book.)

Third -- relying on hyper-analysis. In a business that is often data-driven, there is a strong temptation to forego common sense (related to gut instinct and intuition) in favor of the latest "facts and figures" and their attendant analyses by largely self-anointed experts.

We are all familiar with the phrase, "paralysis by analysis," because it has become somewhat overused and trite. But it conveys an essential truth: hyper-analysis prohibits or inhibits the exercise of gut instincts about trends and trades, opportunities and options. Given our desire to present clients with the absolute best information, there is always a pull toward getting one more piece of data, one more exquisite insight.

Honestly! There will always be new and exciting opinions about how to maximize gains for our clients. But sifting out, sorting through and carefully assessing every bit of new information is essentially a fool's game – akin to market-timing – and we need at some point to go with our gut instincts about what is best and prudent.

I know people in our industry who try to set up pros and cons whiteboards to determine what products to consider, what options to pursue. Ultimately, this technique is doomed to failure since there are always fresh considerations that turn the whiteboard into a balance-board, and the conversation tends to revert to, "let's go with the tried and true," or, "we've always done it this way," or, "experts agree." In the very worst scenario, such an approach inclines us to encourage a client toward the product we most want to sell.

In relation to every client you have, you are the key player. Each and every person relies upon you for achieving their hopes. They trust that you will do the hard analyses, go through the grunt work of digesting and projecting financial information in order to come up with a plan. And bottom line, that plan needs to be based not only on an accumulation of data but also on a gut instinct assessment of what should be set in place. If this were not so, clients would have their needs addressed by logarithms rather than through conversations with us.

Paying heed to the three cautions I have named does not mean valuing instinct over information. That is not what I am advocating. Rather, I am urging you to process all information intuitively. Bluntly, your intuition, your instinct, your "feel" should be considered and valued. As with every decision you make in a business context, ethical requirements and product-specific knowledge assume priority positions, but gut-generated creativity absolutely complements these.

Although there are, to my knowledge, no continuing education courses (Gut Instinct 101) or ways to obtain professional certification (Master of Business Intuition) in the skills I am commending. But there are ways to improve these skills.

## Try these....

> Tune in to tone. At various times in our lives, we have all heard someone say to us or to another person something along the lines of: "I heard what you said but I didn't understand the tone of your voice," or, "You better change your tone if you expect me to listen!" Those phrases capture something essential... how something gets said definitely affects meaning. A cheery, "Hi!" conveys that the speaker is probably having a good day; a sullen, "Hi," may indicate that the greeting is offered as a joyless obligation. How the phrase, "I'll get to that as soon as possible," gets spoken can tell us whether the task will be dealt with promptly or whether we will have to hound the speaker for action. Even how we hear the words, "I love you," is tone-dependent (amorous? casual? encouraging? tossed-off? hollow? etc.).
>
> Having severe visual difficulties as a child made me especially sensitive to reading the tones of voices around me. Listening in this way – tuning in to tone – is something we can all develop as a skill. In effect, it is training ourselves to hear the intent and to identify the emotional content of the words being spoken. We should try purposefully to

become able to identify instances when the meaning of the words we hear from a client seem out of sync with the message conveyed by tone. This is a warning to heed, a point at which clarification needs attention. Positive words and angry tone? Hopeful words and fearful tone? In these and other such cases, gut instinct raises a caution flag. To ignore that intuitive warning is perilous and to follow it is, we discover, likely to be productive and to lead to better future interactions with the client.

Pay attention to body language. This is the visual equivalent to tuning in to tone, so I won't belabor the point. It is well established that our bodies communicate our thoughts, intentions, reactions and emotions in ways that are quite readable to a trained observer. There are countless books available about the subject and I recommend reviewing some in order to gain a general knowledge. Read enough to feel confident that you are a better observer and that you have developed a bit of interpretive skill.

I do not think it especially helpful to micro-analyze clients' postures or movements. It can get a bit weird if we find ourselves thinking, "I hear what she's saying about her financial goals but the way she's holding her pinkie makes me wonder!" Optimally, when we know the basics of what clients' bearing and gestures indicate about their comfort level, we can be more intentional and focused in setting them at ease. Productive conversation requires freely flowing give-and-take; body language serves us well when it provides indicators as to whether or not that is happening.

Both verbal and visual cues can inform us. We are wise to become adept at understanding what both have to say.

Develop a level of trust in your gut instincts. Most of us are quite comfortable with trusting our senses. "Seeing is believing." "I'll never forget that smell." "I know what I heard." "That tasted just like the cookies Grandma made." "I touched it myself so I know it's real."

And, though research is providing some amazing new insights, we still accept the stimulus-response information provided by our five senses as more reliable than that produced by our gut instinct. Fair enough. But perhaps it helps to consider that gut instinct, though not a physical sense, merits being defined as an <u>inner sensitivity</u>.

Just as there are exercises and programs to sharpen the use of our physical senses, there are ways to become more aware of how our personal gut instinct/intuition operates and informs us. A first step is to think of times when we felt guided by gut instinct in ways that proved beneficial. Identifying the characteristics of these events gives us valuable information about when we might find gut instinct especially trustworthy. (Were the clues verbal, visual or both? What amount of data gathering preceded our eventual decision or choice? Was following gut instinct accompanied by a feeling of satisfaction? Did intuition open up a new insight into a problem? These and questions you formulate yourself help define your own distinctive style of using gut instinct in your work and in your personal life.)

One of the most tangible ways that gut instinct has contributed to my own business success is by helping me develop my client list. Sometimes I get an inner sense that I do not want to have a business relationship with someone because he or she conveys an energy-sapping negativity. I feel that in my gut. Honestly, I am not at my best when dealing with such a person, so it benefits both of us to have him or her seek another advisor. To serve such a client ethically and well is to let go. Working against our own gut instinct is never wise and rarely produces a positive outcome. Further, I have learned over the course of my career that there are always other clients with whom I can build strong, successful, productive, positive, mutually satisfying relationships.

A couple closing notes…. Though gut instincts tend to arise spontaneously and often in pressure situations, in a business context they seldom have to be acted upon immediately. In fact, I have found that by allowing them some inner space and a stretch of time, they either expand or contract in impact. I heartily recommend creating a context/environment where you can reflect upon your gut instincts in a relaxed manner. You will find, I believe, that through quiet, effortless internal processing, they will intensify or fade; either way, you will have clearer guidance.

Finally, if you feel that your gut instinct let you down in some situation or transaction, learn to let it go. Dwelling on what you consider an intuitive misfire is as unproductive as pining over an item you sold at a yard sale. Assess the experience for sure, but do not let it deter you from being attentive to gut instincts in the future.

I suspect that in years ahead we will be hearing some astonishing things about gut instincts from scientific researchers. For now, let's learn to use it – each in our own unique way – as a useful item to have in our business tool-kit. I have done so with a high degree of success, and my gut instinct tells me that **if I can do it, you can, too!**

# 6. "Always Selling"

Selling can be considered an art, a science, a social skill. To be good at it requires creativity, precision and confidence in interpersonal contacts. In some form, selling and buying have been around ever since someone with an, "I want/need" feeling engaged in a satisfactory transaction with someone in the position of, "I have what you want/need." This first salesperson and client – call them Og and Bazu – engaged in a transfer in which each received something of value. That simple social contract that Og and Bazu agreed upon started something big, something essential to the maintenance, progress and well-being of our human community.

Beyond this fanciful conjecture about Og and Bazu, we get to the simple fact: selling – the provision of goods or services – has established itself as an essential component of modern cultures and economies. If you are reading this book, it is probable that you are now involved in, or are considering becoming involved in, selling as a profession. I hope that this chapter provides you with some insights that encourage you on your way.

Let's take a brief look at two periods in history that provide groundwork for my first and most important point about engaging in a successful sales career.

Back in the Middle Ages, a common salesperson-presence was the peddler who moved from village to village with his wares (yes, at the time, this was pretty much an all male deal!). To be sure, there were village markets, but the peddlers often brought in their travel chests items that seldom showed up there. Or they brought things on which they could offer "below market prices." Whatever they offered – helpful kitchen items, unusual pieces of fabric or clothing, useful tools, semi-luxuries from foreign lands – they depended on establishing a clientele. Many peddlers made a circuit of villages on a semi-regular basis, and those who did needed to make sure that they provided goods of acceptable quality at a fair cost.

Some peddlers, especially those who showed up seemingly out of nowhere with an odd collection of items, were truly unsavory characters who made people wary of peddlers in general. They might have articles of poor quality or charge inflated prices. Some acquired their merchandise by thievery. They would steal items from residents at one stop and then hustle off to sell them to folks in a village down the road! For a peddler to be assured a warm welcome when he arrived with his chest of stuff to sell, he needed to have established a record of honest dealing in quality goods. Reputation was key. It gave access, allowed for continuity in client relationships, and went a long way toward assuring success.

The mid-twentieth century was the heyday of the traveling salesperson (yes, there were now some women active in the profession). Companies relied on salespersons to provide potential clients with information about products and to present it in a manner that led to orders. Those attempting to cultivate clients had to be engaging, knowledgeable and convincing if they were to achieve a high degree of sales productivity.

These salespersons often worked sizeable territories and racked up massive amounts of miles. In times pre-dating electronic devices that contain huge amounts of data, they regularly carried spec books, samples, pictures and brochures, and a significant amount of information stored in their heads. For companies, those on their traveling sales team functioned as point-persons for customer relations. They were often the ones who answered questions, fielded complaints, gave a face and personality to a company. Salespersons were responsible for cementing an ongoing relationship, and in order to do that they had to exhibit a consistently high level of competence and integrity. Reputation was key. It was a necessity for sustaining access and achieving success.

This foray into sales history is not just a commentary on things gone by. Peddlers were actually pioneers in the area of retail sales, precursors of contemporary on-line sales where items show up at our homes. And there are still millions who follow in the footsteps of last century's traveling sales-persons, though now with substantial and enormously helpful technological options/support. My reason for delving into the past is to make a point that has been true through time, remains true now, and will be true in days to come: Whenever and whatever people are selling, reputation is key. Key to gaining and maintaining client access. Key to reaching high levels of success.

In the remainder of this chapter, I'll be providing you with suggestions for building a sterling reputation. These suggestions, when put into practice, actually create a satisfying and fulfilling lifestyle, something that goes along with my belief that we are always selling.

Years ago, I attended a Million Dollar Round Table event in San Fran-cisco that featured John Savage, a legend in our business. At this "Night With John Savage," one of the attendees asked, "What do I do when someone approaches me with a business question at a social event… out of context?" And the reply was, "What you haven't learned yet is that you're always selling." That was a profound response. It was not, I believe, saying that we should always be ready to talk about policies or products. In the questioner's case, it would mean being courteous, showing interest, possibly sharing contact information or setting up an appointment. In all situations, being in the "always selling" mode means developing your reputation as a person with whom someone would want to do business. Bottom line, it means being a genuine and authentic person at all times and in all circumstances. See! A lifestyle.

A reputation gets built over time through specific actions and behav-iors There are key character traits that need to be developed and refined in order to enable these actions/behaviors. I've identified these as the "Six A's," the half-dozen focus-points that are essential to establishing a solid reputa-tion. They are the ability to be: approachable, alert, accommodating, asser-tive, attentive and appreciative. These comprise a compellingly positive and powerful package of character traits.

1. Be Approachable -- If clients do not implicitly trust you to deal with extraordinary needs as they arise, you have not established yourself

as someone who is non-judgmentally and openly approachable. Our goal is to meet any need with the most effective response possible. This may require some extraordinary extensions of service. Some time back, a long-time client approached me with a unique and challenging situation. His daughter had become pregnant by an older celebrity, a major film star. The father called me to address the situation by writing a life insurance policy on the star that made him the beneficiary so he could provide for his daughter. This request led to a trip to California, a serious issue-specific conversation with the celeb, and a ride around town in his ridiculously expensive car. It all worked out as my client had hoped.... He called me because I had built a <u>reputation</u> for being approachable, for being someone who would address need without judgment and who would place client interest first. When my client had an issue, he identified me as the "go to" option. That is approachability.

2. Be Alert -- Whether driving, attending children, participating in sports or engaging in business activities, it is always wise to be alert. In the context of always selling, this means being aware of all the common interests or causes that connect you to persons with whom you have contact. In our business/profession, connections lead to clients. I'll give you an example. While flying home from a business meeting (I suggest always flying first class for the explicit reason of gaining higher-end contacts), I sat next to a fellow who chose to watch a sequence of old "Tonight Show" broadcasts featuring Johnny Carson. My antennae tuned in. I conversed with him about his interest, got contact info, and spoke with him about an old classmate who had worked for Johnny Carson. Over the next months, I sent him a set of DVDs of Johnny Carson Christmas shows. And because I was alert to his interests, he in turn became interested in my expertise.... the result has been the establishment of a significant source of business. Common interests abound. It takes alertness to identify them.

I'll use this particular example as a segue into asserting that it is important to develop yourself as a person of eclectic interests – someone interested in everything! Build for yourself a reputation for being what I call a "Velcro-person," someone who seems able to attach to everyone. This is a valuable and doable and enjoyable professional goal. When you exhibit interest in and knowledge about subjects raised by others, you become increasingly approachable on many levels. Does this take work and intentional study – yes. Is it worth the effort – absolutely.

3. Be Accommodating -- Accommodating clients basically comes down to combining knowledge with empathy. All customer service starts with the coupling of knowledge and empathy. Know what services you can provide and feel yourself into the client's situation. The word accommodate comes from Latin roots meaning "to do something in a fitting and suitable manner." Isn't that what service is?... responding to any inquiry for assistance by providing what fits the problem and addresses it with a suitable solution.

A few years ago, a client called me with an unusual request. His son was involved in a very dangerous sport as his career. He called me because he knew only one company could insure his son and he thought I might have a connection. While this was certainly outside my usual range of policy-writing, I was able to establish the necessary connection and provide coverage of a life insurance policy. The relieved father/client called me and said, in words I could entirely understand, "Thank you. I hope I never have to talk with you again."

Yet because I knew some of his other needs and concerns, I continued to send him materials (flyers, letters, updates, etc.). This may seem old-fashioned in a way, but tangible "keep contact" stuff does indicate thoughtfulness and concern. Over time, his wife -- who opened all the mail – contacted me for additional business. She did this because I had established with them a reputation for accommodating their specific needs. I had simply exercised my knowledge and tailored it to provide an empathetic response.

4. Be Assertive -- Please follow me carefully on this. By being assertive, I do not mean following the stereotype of the "foot-in-the-door" salesperson nor do I advocate the kind of sales techniques that are more

berating than educating. We do not want clients to feel they have succumbed to an assault; we want them to feel they have succeeded with a plan. Assertiveness is not aggressiveness. Assertiveness is born of confidence while aggressiveness is a product of fear.

There is a huge difference between saying, "We can solve your problem," versus, "You've got to get this product." The former implies engaging in a mutual effort. The latter projects something distastefully forceful. I believe that a good indicator of appropriate assertiveness is to see if it meets the "we" test. To assert: "We can put together something that can meet your needs," is far different from, "I have the answer to your needs." To be effective, assertiveness needs to be an expression of mutual effort/decision. There is no finer reputation to establish than to be tagged as a collaborative partner. Assertiveness at its best involves collaborative understandings.

5. Be Attentive -- What person does not want to have some attention paid to him/her? Perhaps a confirmed recluse, but the vast majority of folks desire enough attention from other to verify, "I'm worthy/valued/noticed."

Earlier in my career, I inherited an "orphan client" from another agent who had retired. I began treating him as a regular client although I had never done business with him. I sent birthday and appropriate holiday cards, updates on products and services, materials describing my business. Over several years, this fellow never checked the box on my brochures next to the words, "I would like you to contact me." But one day that changed, and I responded promptly. He had just won a sizeable amount of money in a lottery and I began working with him on investing the winnings in a wise fashion. He called upon me because I had provided clear and continuous information, because I had established with him a reputation for attentiveness.

I average eighteen contacts annually with every client I have. In addition to holiday and birthday cards, descriptions of my services and pertinent updates on products, I initiate a goal-setting session around the start of a new year or on the anniversary of the client's business relationship with me.

For local clients, I also keep my eye out for positive pieces in the media that mention them; I send along a copy with a brief note. Making all these contacts is not difficult, costly or especially time-consuming. It simply requires organization and discipline.

Attentiveness is more than just the extension of courtesy, though that is an important and welcomed component. It is what clients deserve. We are relied upon to be, in fact, a client's personal attendant in relation to some of the most significant financial decisions he or she will ever make. Our attentiveness helps solidify our reputations as persons who are responsive and trustworthy.

6. Be Appreciative -- In real estate, people say that the key components of a good site are, "Location, location, location." In sales, we can say that the key components of building a good sales relationship are, "Thank you, thank you, thank you." We are, to be blunt, completely dependent on clients for our success, and it is both smart and honest to acknowledge that to them. I let my clients know on a regular basis that I appreciate them. I thank them for their trust, their questions, their business, their referrals and, yes, their friendship. Although this may seem quaint and old-fashioned, I am a firm believer in hand-written thank you notes. In a world where we think "time is money" or gripe about not having enough time, a hand-written thank you conveys that my level of appreciation has moved me to send something of value, something into which I invested time and effort. And ask yourself… If you received a stack of mail that contains one hand-written envelope, are you not likely to open that first? (Note – There is no downside personally or professionally to establishing a reputation as someone who is thoughtfully appreciative.)

Those who help us in our outreach to clients and in the day-to-day operations of our business also need to know how much we appreciate them. With vendors, a simple way of expressing this is something I have done consistently: I pay them first before anything else comes out of income. In turn, they appreciate that I appreciate what they provide, and the practice helps build a reputation for promptness and fairness. Staff, too, needs to be thanked and commended. I freely acknowledge that my staff does all the things I either cannot do, do not want to do or would do with less efficiency. The manner you express appreciation to staff is personal choice; doing so is an essential.

What I say next may seem a bit "out there"… or maybe "in there." In short, I'm advocating the practice of appreciative reflection. Specifically, I believe that it is uplifting to take some time for reflection upon the opportunities our profession gives us to succeed personally, to be of service to clients and community. I grew up just shy of poor and now it is common for me to write policies of immense value. I am grateful to my profession for giving me a context for achievement. Early in my life, I had no confidence in my vision of a future. I am grateful that the practice of my profession has challenged me with the notion that, "You don't change until your thinking changes," and that it has rewarded my evolution to new ways of thinking with ample success. It is an absolute positive to live in a spirit of well-considered gratitude. It is also a great antidote to the stress that can poison our lives.

This notion that we are always selling does not mean that we are constantly marketing products that bring us income; we are not always lugging around a portfolio of contracts and investment proposals. In truth, the most important product we offer is inescapably present, and it has an immense intangible value – ourselves. As with other professionals (physicians, attorneys, retailers, teachers, athletes, etc.), our greatest offerings to others are the things that define who we are: our skills, our expertise, our trustworthiness, our ability to provide access to needed goods or products, our empathy, our ethics, our energy, and yes, our reputation.

Attaining and maintaining a reputation to be proud of is a process that calls for disciplined thoughtfulness and ongoing effort. For me, it has meant paying attention to lots of "little things"… being up to speed on current events, keeping an even demeanor, dressing well for social or civic events, staying physically fit. I strive to be someone people enjoy being around as an acquaintance, companion or friend. Professionally, of course, it serves me well to become someone it's hard to say "No" to! What I'm saying is that I do not get to that position by being annoying, coercive or insistent. Happily, my best professional identity coincides with who I want to be at my genuine best. I want to be likeable, knowledgeable, easy to talk to, empathetic when hearing others' problems, someone who is "more interested than interesting." One of the things I love about our profession is that we serve our clients best when we <u>are</u> our best.

What I hope you carry from this chapter is an excitement about creating a sterling reputation and keeping it untarnished. To adopt the "6 A's" as traits you have at your very core means, I believe, that you will find yourself in possession of a highly satisfying lifestyle as well. It will be a lifestyle that prepares you for success.

I do want to acknowledge that the concept of always selling may strike you as relentlessly demanding or burdensome. I confess that there are times when I feel, as one friend phrased it, "peopled out." We will be addressing this and offering some remedies and positive practices in the chapter on, "Balance."

I did not enter a sales career with strong financial backing or high-light-reel skills, but I learned that building a <u>reputation</u> has more to do with intention than means, more to do with goals than perceived limitations. Commitment to the "6 A's" is key. No question – <u>if I can do it, you can, too</u>!

# 7. "Balance"

Consider the importance of balance. Early in life, gaining the sense of balance that enables us to walk is a world-expanding physical achievement (and something that changes the lives of parents immediately and decisively!). In some professions, maintaining balance is a life or death issue. Tight-rope walkers and construction workers on skyscrapers must maintain balance at all costs. For athletes, a combination of strength, speed and balance is essential for success. Baseball pitchers speak of attaining a "balance point" before delivering the ball to home plate and gymnasts perform on a piece of equipment called a balance beam. Coaches in team sports generally seek to assemble a productive balance of offense and defense. Medical professionals have long identified chemical imbalances within a person as causative factors of physical illness or mental health issues. Nationally or individually, there are significant reasons to work towards constructing a balanced budget. And a balanced diet… well, many of us try to adhere to one through our eating choices. In short, it shouldn't take an announcement from an ER staffer after a traumatic event – "His/her life is in the balance!" – to alert us to the fact that balance is something crucial for us to define, understand and achieve…. I'll be getting back to that exclamatory phrase at the close of this chapter.

There are a multitude of examples I could use illustrating the importance of balance to human health and behavior, but instead I'm going to use a mechanical image that may be more universally understood. It makes the point. All, or most of us, drive automobiles. Let's imagine that your car has a misaligned front end. Something – worn tires, malfunctioning shocks, faulty ball joints, etc. – causes an imbalance. On you drive. The more you drive, the more the problems amplify. Handling the car becomes increasingly difficult. Your ability to address challenging traffic situations or crises diminishes. Bumps in the road throw you off course. The more you ignore the imbalance, the more dire the consequences become. You lose control. Eventually you cannot safely or responsibly move ahead at all. Imbalance imperils. And as with an automotive journey on paved roads, so a lack of personal balance impairs or impedes our progress as we navigate the course of our life.

OK, OK. You have probably heard from many sources the benefits of leading a balanced lifestyle. I acknowledge and applaud that, but I want to offer what I hope will be meaningful additions to the concept of balance as it relates to the practice of our profession. Even as I encourage you to work hard and to recognize the "always selling" aspect of what we do, I'll be lobbying hard for you to adopt a broad and, I believe, profoundly life-enhancing approach to balance.

Our initial task – if we are to convert the concept of balance from a noble notion into practical actions – is to define the areas in which we will focus our attention and commitment. In other words, what are we trying to balance? Over the years, I've identified four pairs of balance-point challenges. They are:

Acquisition – Dispersal

Interaction – Solitude

Organization – Exploration

Business – Beyond

These pairs have formed the core of my efforts to create the balanced life necessary for keeping on course personally and professionally. I'll share briefly how I have come to understand and work with them. I am quite confident you will be able to adapt them to your particular goals and circumstances.

## Acquisition and Dispersal

When I consider improving my personal life and my professional capabilities, I do not think about acquiring "stuff" at all. What I seek out are things that increase my energy level, improve my health, enhance my mental sharpness – these are the possessions that lead to a more fulfilling life, a more successful career.

At the risk of sounding boring or parental or trite, I want to make a strong statement about paying attention to diet and exercise. You can check out a multitude of scientific studies if you wish corroboration, but I simply assert from experience: when I exercise regularly and when I eat wisely, I feel better and I perform better for my clients. I leave it to you to check out the benefits of producing endorphins and judiciously increasing heart rate, of monitoring eating schedules and carefully planning menus. And tack on a postscript to wrestle with: I have learned that realizing the full benefits of things that make me more energy-filled and robust is effective only when I set aside those things that deplete me. For many of us, this will mean minimizing an intake of alcohol (clinically a depressant) and avoiding any toxins identifiable in food. Again, your own research and discernment of comfort levels is key.

On the intellectual level, I encourage you to be voraciously curiosity-driven. Read, read, read. Whatever knowledge you acquire – in areas of products/sales or in broader and diversified realms – will help you grow as a person and will build connections with clients. Use the Internet to probe as well, but realize that much "information" available there is suspect and that the behavior identified as "screening" has been designated addictive. Here's a simple test: Do you read and exercise as much as you devote to screen time? If not, pause to reassess.

So… Do you feel positive benefits from your exercise and eating? Are you listening to your body? Are you honing your intellectual skills, keeping your mind sharp or letting it dull? Through your activities, habits and disciplines, strive to acquire these things: a reliable supply of energy, an insatiable desire to learn, a sustainable level of health.

All right. Now for the balance. Once you've filled your life with the good things just noted, it's time to start sharing these acquired gifts with others. Dispersing what we acquire not only serves to prevent self-satisfaction or selfishness, it is simply part of the give-and-take that creates a truly satisfying balance in our lives.

When we have "energy to burn," we can certainly use it to fuel our business efforts where endurance means reaching more clients and having the ability to "go the extra mile" for them. It also means being a more active participant as parent or partner or community member. Parenting, partnering and volunteering become positive outlets for expending energy, whereas with a depleted supply of energy we too often regard them negatively as drains upon us.

The stockpile of knowledge that we build up through reading or other forms of inquiry serves as a resource for engaging in conversations with others. When the information we acquire is business or product specific, we become for clients a personal access-point for what they need to know. This is obviously advantageous as a means of gaining trust. But also, when we can offer informed comments about a wide variety of subjects, we have an enhanced ability to connect with others on the basis of their interests… a guaranteed relationship-builder. Acquiring knowledge can be great fun, and it is a basic source of competence and confidence. Dispersing knowledge with sensitivity and humility is the essence of wisdom; it allows us to be wiser as parents, partners, citizens and client advisors.

At a core level, our health as a human being is based on an essential balance of acquisition and dispersal. We call it breathing. We acquire required oxygen through the intake of air and we let out unneeded carbon dioxide by breathing out. Acquire. Disperse. Inhale. Exhale. A beautiful balance. I believe that by paying careful attention to the points covered above, you will be able to achieve a sense of balance that will feel like a new breath of life.

## Interaction and Solitude

Our profession is grounded in the belief that by providing specific plans and products, we can help persons attain their financial goals and realize some of their fondest hopes. Our profession generally draws "people-persons," those who enjoy interacting with others and being of service to them. In fact, if you do not enjoy these things you might want to do a career reassessment!

That said, dealing with people also presents us with our greatest challenges. A friend who worked for decades in a service profession had a phrase for this. He said there were times when he just got "peopled out." The truth is that constant interaction takes a toll. I'll use another mechanical image that might be helpful…. Whenever two physical objects in motion are in constant contact, they wear on each other. There's an abrasiveness that affects – and diminishes – both. In a worst case scenario, the friction between the two can become so heated that they can burn out. In our case, contact with people that is too much, too fast, too close can cause us to reach that state my friend tagged as "peopled out." And if we get to that point, we are ineffective and unhappy.

To extend my image a bit, we can note that proper lubrication with oil, silicon, graphite, etc. can greatly mitigate the undesirable effects of constant contact. These substances serve to inhibit wear, improve efficiency and, in the case of engines and such, prolong life. So – can we identify what it is that serves the same purpose for our contacts and interactions within the realm of business? I believe that the three essential "lubricants," the things that I must bring into my professional interactions if I want them to move easily and in a productive way are these: energy, positive attitude and relaxation. There are, I've discovered, ways I can nurture smoother interpersonal contact. I commend them to you. They can be identified as the manners of interaction and practices of solitude set forth in the following paragraphs.

Nothing has helped me keep up a high level of energy for client contact more than establishing a clear, consistent set of boundaries. I have set periods of times when I'm available and times when I'm not. If it seems counterintuitive to restrict access in service to being more productive and client friendly, I understand the bewilderment! But consider this…. When clients do get in touch with me (and my times are suitably generous), they know that I will be entirely present for them; I will be eager and energized and engaged; I will not be in a rushed or distracted state; I will let my time be their time. Given these benefits that clients sense, I have found that they appreciate and respect the boundaries I set. They understand them as part of my professional approach, as a way of defining our shared time as valuable.

Here's something else that has kept me enthusiastic about interactions with clients. I devote a good deal of time to developing a profile of model clients. These are persons about whom I would almost assuredly and immediately have a positive attitude. I imagine and describe (in written form) the characteristics, ages, needs, values, occupations of persons I would most like to work with and be most effective in assisting. Then… I am quite intentional about seeking out such people. Selecting a client base on this criterion of "most-likely-to-attach" is not only wise but also time-saving and business-savvy. This selection process is not inhibiting or limiting; it is invigorating and liberating. When we attach ourselves to persons with whom we have much in common, our interaction is likely to have productive results.

Because we are involved deeply and often in the lives of others in ways that make strenuous use of our interpersonal skills/understandings, we need the balance provided by intentional times of solitude. This is, I want to state firmly, a necessity and not a luxury. We cannot make the mistake of considering solitude as time that is wasted, unproductive or empty. This would be as wrong-headed as deeming dull-looking tons of gold ore as worthless without recognizing the glittering value they contain. Solitude is somewhat like smelting… it helps us discover and refine what is valuable within ourselves. Fear of solitude is often related to a lack of self-confidence, to an uneasy feeling that we might find ourselves dull through-and-through, to a sense that our worth is dependent on the opinions of others. It is a fear or hesitation that, when faced and overcome, both enriches us and makes us more engaging in personal interactions.

The practice of solitude involves some seeming paradoxes. It requires that we make the effort to be relaxed. It asks us to take the time to step away from being ruled by time. It calls us to trust that we can be alone without being lonely. That last point is key. The twentieth-century writer May Sarton put it concisely when she stated, "Loneliness is the poverty of the self; solitude is the richness of self." Solitude is that time/space in which we truly discern who we are. It is our way of "keeping company with ourselves," and if somehow we find that stressful or boring, it can be a sharp warning about how we might be coming across to others. If we enjoy our opportunities for solitude, it's a good sign that we have A) an active mind, B) a composed approach to life, and C) a comfort with honest self-assessment and reflection. The acquisition of these ABC's should be a goal of our solitary times.

Solitude allows us to develop our pursuit of avocations (literally, those things we do when not at work). The range of activities that fall into this category is almost endless and the selection of particular ones that best suit us is a matter of personal choice. (I will, however, share some thoughts when I speak later in this chapter about "exploration.") I do want to make a general recommendation that you include in your solitary activities those that engage you in a variety of ways… aerobic exercise, concentrated study, unencumbered contemplation, "mindless" entertainments, immersion in nature, etc. This variety helps you to experience numerous ways of learning, of achieving a better level of health, of expanding your spirit/inner self, of gaining self-awareness and self-appreciation and self-reliance. The eighteenth-century Irish writer Laurence Sterne noted that, "In solitude the mind gains strength and learns to lean upon itself." If anything, Sterne understates it…. Well-practiced solitude improves the fitness of our entire selves.

I value my solitary times of jogging in a serene environment, reading, listening to music, watching a humorous movie or using exercise equipment. And I've developed a few methods of assuring that I secure these. You can institute your own, but mine might serve as helpful examples. First, every day I schedule a number of mini-breaks during work hours. These serve as brief time-outs, periods equivalent to the time-outs in athletic events that allow for rest/recuperation and for planning future strategy. Second, I have an unlisted personal phone number. This, quite obviously, permits an effective vocation/avocation separation. Third, I get regular sleep (the ultimate solitude!). Scientific research has firmly established that we require significant stretches of unbroken sleep to recharge our bodies, to allow our brains a period of uninterrupted and uninhibited creativity. Monitoring and establishing your own effective sleep patterns is a prime commitment to productive solitude.

In summary, solitude is the gestation period for bringing to life your best self in interaction with others.

## Organization and Exploration

In the history of the United States (and other nations, too), there have been areas designated as "unorganized territories." These were places about which much was unknown, places where norms and laws and standards of behavior were often loosely adhered to or ignored. If we are to achieve success in our profession, our workplace – in terms of schedules and structures, patterns and practices – cannot be unorganized territory.

In our lives outside the business context, we may not enjoy creating fixed schedules of activities or having everything in its place or adhering to set routines and methods of operation. We savor a sense of serendipity, of going with the flow, of changing plans, of doing what we feel like doing, of adopting a leisurely pace. These approaches absolutely provide a balance that I'll be addressing in the next part of the chapter. But for now, let's focus on everyday workplace organization.

Here's a take-it-to-the-bank statement: In our business, organization is essential; it is organization that enables efficiency and effectiveness. The obvious tasks of organization are, of course, things we likely have in place… having a reliable process for retrieving client information and records, having clearly defined and skill-specific roles for staff members, having a set of contingency plans for emergencies or absences, having stated policy regarding legal/ethical behavior. These are basic organizational necessities for any office (so if you don't have them in place, start there!).

The goal of just about any organizational techniques or structures is to maximize the availability of productive time. Time is, after all, the one resource we have in a fixed quantity. I have two practices, both of which I commend to you, that help me best use this limited asset. The first is that I have a strict schedule. I have a set time to arrive for work and (importantly!) a set time to leave. This creates a work situation not unlike that of an athlete competing in a game that has a fixed amount of playing time. Just as with the athlete, I commit my best effort and ability and judgment and focus within that limited time period. Are there occasional "overtimes" brought on by extraordinary circumstances? Of course, but these are quite rare. And if we schedule in prudent "time-outs," empty spaces in the daily schedule, they become exceedingly rare.

The second practice I urge you to consider is one I have already noted, but it is important enough to merit reiteration and extension: Set the times when you are accessible and when you are not. I won't rehash the benefits of this that I previously explained, but I mention it again because it serves as the prime example of interruption-avoidance. Whatever you can do to organize your work environment in ways that minimize interruptions, give that high priority. There have been numerous studies designed to show the cost in lost time caused by interruptions. It has been estimated that it takes up to nine minutes following a one-minute interruption fully to regain one's focus and flow of thought. Interruption is the enemy of productivity.

One of the greatest general lessons I ever learned about the importance of organization came in the year that I ran for a statewide public office, a venture I'll write about in more detail later. During that year while I was campaigning, I hired a driver so I could work while traveling to engagements, a staff addition I have maintained and a move I highly endorse. I also delegated much more work to office staff who discovered new areas of competence as I let go of things others could do as well (or better!) than I. I made sure all communications systems and procedures were clear and smooth-running. Amidst all these modifications and major changes – a kind of exercise in tightening efficiency – I had fears that my business would suffer. In fact, I/we had our best year ever by far and morale stayed at peak level. I gained valuable new wisdom about organization.

We can think of organizational efforts as like the bones and internal organs of our bodies, those things that give our business its structure and ability to function. They are not, however, what is most visible to clients. It is our own presence, perceptiveness and personality that attract and engage them. And for that reason, we need to flesh ourselves out by adding to the discipline of organization the balance of some fulfilling, free-ranging exploration.

What I'm encouraging you to do is to follow these joyful recommendations.... Have some fun. Be uninhibitedly imaginative. Push your limits. Savor serendipity. Discover new talents. In short, explore your interests and expand your range of curiosity.

Just as physical exploration leads to an expansion of known territory, so the exploration I'm promoting gives you an expanded knowledge of yourself and the world. For the purposes of this chapter, I'm recommending that you choose to stretch yourself gently into comfortable and relaxing activities. I'll have more to say about pushing beyond your "comfort zone" in a later chapter. Here are four areas to consider for some easy exploration.

1. Exercise – Although I've already discussed reasons for exercise, I want to urge you to explore the range of exercise options available to you. Team and individual. Indoors and outdoors. Calming and sweat-inducing. The point of pursuing a number of exercise activities is that they challenge/strengthen your body in a variety of ways, they call for diverse interactions with others, and, as shown in a number of scientific studies, they call upon your mind to think in a wide range of patterns.

2. Hobbies -- A hobby is a purely interest-driven activity. Whatever you choose, it will likely bring enjoyment, increase your ability to plan and concentrate, and help define who you are as a unique individual. So... crocheting to crosswords, baking to bird watching, stamp collecting to studying Sumerian pottery. Go for it!

3. Spirituality -- Whatever this word means to you, the bigger-and-beyond-self realm merits exploration. Call it exercise for our inner being in service to gaining new perspectives on all that surrounds us. I have participated in classic religious training, yoga sessions, nature immersions, practices of silence and mindfulness. Each has contributed to a deeper understanding of myself and others.

4. Travel -- Beyond giving us a genuine appreciation for places beyond our familiar environment and for other cultures or ways of life, travel

provides points of connection with new acquaintances/clients. To discover, "Hey, we've both been to the same place," is an immediate conversation starter. I believe that making a commitment to travel as much as possible (choose extensiveness over expensiveness!) is imperative. It helps us to value diversity. Generally, the broader our travel, the broader our minds.

## Business and Beyond

This balance-point pairing is one that concentrates on our achieving positive experiences both in the context of work and in the range of activities that comprises the rest of our lives. As best we can, we should aim at creating a thoroughgoing win-win situation. If we pull this off, our living become thriving.

Steve Jobs, who founded one of the premier businesses of all time, Apple, had a keen insight into what makes for a satisfying personal work experience. He said this:

"Your work is going to fill a large part of your life, and the only way to be truly satisfied is to do what you believe is great work. And the only way to do great work is to love what you do. If you haven't found it yet, keep looking. Don't settle. As with all matters of the heart, you'll know when you find it."

Steve Jobs endorses a following of gut instinct (note the chapter on that in this book) when establishing a career. I can honestly say that I love the work I do, and I want to share some of the ways I keep that love alive.

Playing off the notion that "absence makes the heart grow fonder," I intentionally leave my office for a few days every couple months. This is an exercise in letting go, in humbly recognizing the limits of my "essentialness," in trusting my staff, in honing my skills of delegating responsibilities and defining the work to be done. Risky? If carefully done, not really. Rewarding? Absolutely, for I return with renewed excitement for the work I do.

I have also found it essential to become comfortable with saying "no" when needed and with allowing some work to go "undone." This is neither an exercise in negativity nor a cave-in to laziness. There is a strategic wisdom to saying "no" to an enticing piece of great business when it would over-stress a schedule or disturb regular/required contacts. Put in blunt terms, risking a fling should not be allowed imperil stable relationships. There are times when "no" can be a positive response when it keeps us on track and away from a high-risk detour. Likewise, leaving things undone can also be a wise and productive choice. To push ourselves to work on a project/task when we are tired or stressed is, flat out, stupid. We may even start resenting having to do the work at hand, and that is a killer of positive creativity and best efforts. Getting something done should always be secondary to doing our work with peak focus and intellectual energy. Lackadaisical or lackluster immediacy does not well serve us or our clients long term.

As an extension of the willingness to leave things undone until a proper time, I've also learned to adopt a perspective of patient serenity when dealing with hot/contentious/challenging issues. The old adage of, "count to ten before responding," is spot on… but sometimes the count needs to be extended to a thousand! When our feelings are in any way enraged, we cannot be effectively engaged. Over-reacting immediately to a difficult or complex situation almost never works out well. Stepping back, letting muddied issues settle and allowing turbulent feelings calm will likely bring a needed clarity. A wise counselor once said to me, "In almost every circumstance or situation in life, you have the luxury of time." Sometimes, in a business environment that gets schedule-driven and fixated on quantities (sales, contacts, contracts, etc.), we think of time as our enemy. It is not. And no one has more of it than anyone else! It is our ally, something we do well to recognize as we work with it and within it.

A final note on career contentment. I am able to absent myself from work because I count on the productive presence of those I have hired. Wise hires are foundation blocks of a successful business. The essentials are these: hire people who respect you and appreciate your expertise, who follow directions but are unhesitant to share ideas, who desire to improve their own skills, who seek to understand and serve the wide-ranging needs of clients, who steadfastly practice patience and courtesy. If I were to identify the multiple reasons why I love to come to work, high on the list would be my rapport with staff and my trust in their abilities.

To get our work-life to a place where we are satisfied with its content and pace is a noble achievement. But, as we all know, there's more to life than work. A recent LinkedIn survey identified the fact that seventy percent of responders named the work/life balance as a major stressor. To me, not a surprise. Thus, this lengthy chapter on balance!

Let me share some math with you… I'll round off the numbers a bit. Let's assume you live for eighty-five years, about 745,000 hours. And let's also assume that you work forty-five years at forty-five hours per week; adding in about ten hours per week for business-related travel, you'll put in about 120,000 hours on the job. We'll allot about 250,000 hours for sleep. With work and sleep accounted for, that leaves more than half your life in the wide-awake "beyond business" realm.

I won't presume to dictate what you need to do with this vast amount of time (though the sections in this chapter on "Dispersal" and "Exploration" offer some suggestions as does the chapter on "Get Out of Your Comfort Zones"). I will state candidly that whatever your choices, they need to contain counterbalances to the stresses, interpersonal demands and time constraints of business life.

A brief mention of three things I have found helpful in making the "beyond business" environment truly a space for re-creation and recon- nection… 1) I make sure that I use a clear, effective communication system with my family and friends when I am not physically present. Knowing that understandings and/or agreements are in place allows us to reconnect with- out delay or impediment when we do get together again. 2) I commit to one day a week that has absolutely no intrusions from business. 3) When I say, "I have left the office," I consider it a statement of fact, not intent.

The immense amount of time "beyond business" is something we need to discern, define, deal with.

This chapter is intentionally placed near the mid-point, the heart, of this book. I understand the lure of devoting enormous amounts of time to a business. Sure, there's always work to be done, another client to contact, another plan to implement. But I know that I became more successful, productive and content when I implemented the seeking of balance as a life strategy both within both my time at work and the expanse of time "beyond business." Achieving the balance that's right for you is the challenge I set before you… a challenge that beckons you to make crucial personal choices and changes. The rewards of meeting this challenge are immense, and I know that **if I can do it, you can, too!**

# 8. "Everyone a Potential Client... or a Source of Inspiration"

To achieve success in sales requires understanding the basic promise – and the core premise – of our business: **every person is a potential client and everyone/everything can be a source of inspiration.** I believe this deeply. It is not something I learned in any particular course or continuing education program. It did not pop up as an instantaneous insight. No one explicitly told me this. Simply and emphatically, experience was my teacher. And the only way you will come to an understanding of the promise/premise I've noted, the only way you will come to appreciate how it holds true for you, will be through thoughtful reflection on your own life experience.

My goal in this chapter is not to lay out a specific course of action or set of steps. What I intend to do is, by sharing some examples from my own career, to help you develop a mind-set and a skill-set that prove useful. So while this chapter will be more narrative in form than most of the others, I hope you will emerge from reading it with some clear ideas that are applicable to your own unique situation. Ideas about how to be more open-minded and open-hearted. Ideas about how to respond to serendipitous events. Ideas about discovering trusted sources for personal growth. Ideas about creating opportunity.

We can begin by affirming, and I trust agreeing, that to varying degrees and at a variety of levels everyone has needs. Obviously, I can never meet the needs of all persons around me and I would be foolish to try. But... by being receptive, by listening and caring, I can discover which persons I can most ably assist through my skills, advice and business services. Welcoming and being **open to all** is the starting point for this discernment process. It is important to communicate in every way possible – through ads, accessibility, attitude, etc. – that being "open for business" truly means being open to everyone. This is crucial… and it must be genuine. No artificial flavoring!

On to some stories. I think they will provide some helpful resources for self-assessment, for personal reflection and for strategic planning.

### "The Potency of Improbability" Client #1

Early in my career, my original rented office area was not optimal in space or arrangement, not entirely conducive to inviting comfort. But we tried to control clutter, jury-rig the placement of office equipment and make it as welcoming as possible. One day, my secretary came in and said, "There's a guy who just walked in who says he wants to talk with you." I cleared off a chair, tidied my desk a bit and waited. The sixty-ish man came in and we shook hands. I noticed he had a firm grip. His clothes were well-worn, his color a bit sallow, his mouth in need of major dental work. He presented several signs of being economically disadvantaged and I confess that I sized him up as an improbable client…. He was about to teach me a lesson, one that I could receive only because I adhered to the essential principles of being open, non-judgmental and service oriented. Looking around my humble office, I smiled to myself and simply felt grateful that someone would walk in to do business.

I listened. I learned as we engaged in conversation that he had worked for decades in an industrial job. He had never married and enjoyed a satisfying yet utterly frugal lifestyle. His issue: the plant where he had worked lifelong was closing down and, with impending unemployment, he needed an assured income. He also informed me that he'd used every opportunity to accumulate company stock that would now have to be cashed in… valued at well over a million dollars. In relatively short order, we created an annuity that enabled him to maintain his chosen and rigorously simple way of life. And he took pleasure in knowing that he'd be leaving substantial gifts to nephews and nieces upon his death.

When this man stepped into my office, it was tempting to think, "This guy couldn't possibly become a major client." But here's the lesson I took away from that encounter, and it's a valuable one for everyone in sales: **don't ever mistake the improbable for the impossible.** Remain open at all times to the potency (and rewards!) of improbability. Improbable clients should make up a significant percentage of your portfolio.

## "The Pursuit of Serendipitous Spin-Offs" Client #2

While settling into my seat for a plane trip home after a business meeting, I got a tap on my shoulder. I looked up and a well-dressed woman said curtly, "I believe you're in my seat." I drew a breath and said, "I'm sorry, but I'm certain it's mine. I always get an aisle seat." She persisted. With a smidgen of annoyance, I opened up my travel bag and pulled out the ticket confirming that I was in the proper seat and that she had the window. Our first interaction was not the greatest inducement to start a conversation, but we made light of the initial contact, exchanged first names, and chatted about where we had been and where we were headed, about news and family and air travel in general. She asked what I did for work, I told her, gave her my card, and she replied, "I think I'll be in touch. I want to get some life insurance on my husband. I'm mostly in Los Angeles and New York but I'm not sure I trust those big-city guys." She smiled. My office, by the way, is in a small Mid-West town. Sure enough, she called, and we began our business relationship with her purchase of the desired life insurance policy. This led to my assisting her with stock purchases. When these did well, she passed my name to her father, a former corporate CEO who had a different set of financial needs. This was a great piece of spin-off business, the kind of word-of-mouth referral that is the best possible advertising.

One day, when I was not feeling well, Client #2 called me at home. Since I was expecting to hear from her, I had instructed the office staff to let her phone me there. She asked what I was doing at home and I replied with a semi-flippant response along the lines of, "Eating bon-bons." She said, "I'm pretty sure you don't know who I am when I'm at work." I was not quite sure what she meant; I knew she was in entertainment, but I make it a practice not to push people to reveal more about themselves than they feel comfortable doing. "Since you're home today, turn on your TV." [She specified a time and channel later in the day.] I watch almost no television but dutifully followed instructions. I discovered that she was a major star on a popular show. I called the next day and said, "How come you never told me that?" Simple answer: "You never asked." I had worked to meet her planning needs and had treated her with the same non-intrusive caring and solid respect I extended to all clients. She had appreciated that. I had served her as my client and not treated her like a star. Because we had established such a strong business relationship, I felt comfortable asking immediately, "Would you introduce me to your agent?" She laughed and said, "Always working, huh, Scott?" and agreed to make the connection if I would fly to the West Coast. That introduction to the agent came with the implicit endorsement of my client, and it led to spin-off business with him and, through him, with others in the entertainment community.

Discovering I had a "star" client was pure serendipity. But the spin-off clients became possible because I recognized the possibilities in the situation presented to me and had developed a strong client relationship that permitted me to ask her assistance. In our business, just about everything good – professional success, reputation, personal satisfaction, financial benefits, friendships – derives from creating solid bonds with clients. This, as I say elsewhere in the book, takes honest hard work. The sons of Neil Armstrong have noted that any one of the Apollo astronauts might have been picked to be the first to walk the moon, something the humble astronaut himself knew. That he was chosen was serendipitous… and he was ready. Son Mark put it beautifully and profoundly: "He worked hard. He prepared himself as best he could for whatever the future might bring him. He used to say that **success is where preparation met opportunity.**" (quoted in Discover, June 2019)

Not one of us will be chosen to wander the moon and few of us will discover a client's stardom, but each one of us has clients who can provide us with serendipitous spin-offs that we can pursue. So…. Work hard. Be alert. And be ready to act with intention and energy when serendipity strikes, when your preparation meets with opportunity.

## "The Importance of Sustained and Consistent Contact"
## Clients #3A and #3B

Back when I was single, I met a vibrant young woman at a social event. We seemed to hit it off and shared conversation about plans and hopes for our careers. She turned down my offer of a date but said, "I might want to buy some life insurance from you. You never know. So keep in touch." I was pleased that she was at least attracted to my trustworthiness! So I chose to maintain a contact that I easily could have let go had I succumbed to petty feelings of rejection. We followed up over time and I provided her and her family with suitable life insurance coverage. Twenty years into our business relationship, she died. Dating Client #3a might have been great. Serving her and knowing that her family would be provided for made our sustained contact a matter of greater significance and satisfaction.

While on a ski trip some time ago, a fellow jumped on the chairlift with me as we headed up for a final run. He was gregarious, high-energy, engaging. When we reached the top, we exchanged a quick, "Enjoy!" and headed downhill. Later that day, I saw this man again in the lodge. We chatted for quite awhile and in the course of conversation I learned that he was an executive in a growing industry. I spoke with him about my business and told him that I'd keep in touch since I'd enjoyed our first meeting and felt I might be helpful to him at some future time. [A brief but important note… My statement that I would continue contact was not an off-handed, toss-away comment. It was much more. "Let's keep in touch" has become such a cheap and largely meaningless phrase that we minimize the importance of enduring/durable communication. My point is a simple one: When we say that we will maintain contact with someone, that we will stay in touch, that needs to be conferred with the status of a firm commitment. Certainly, we don't have to promise ongoing contact to anyone, but when we do, we need to do so purposefully and reliably. It will make us stand out. And it's really just a matter of keeping our word!]

My instinct about the fellow in the chair lift told me that he was a success-story in process and that down the road he would have needs for financial planning that he could not yet even imagine. Every year I sent brief "how're you doing" notes, holiday cards, information updating him on my business and its offerings. Eight years after our meeting on the slope, I received a phone call from him seeking to establish a business relationship, his needs now being some of the things I had intuited. Cumulatively, over the years between meeting and call, I had put in fewer than ten hours of work keeping contact, and Client #3B had interpreted my communications as I intended them – not as a pesky persistence than can seem predatory but rather as the caring consistency I had promised. Never undervalue follow-through with your clients. And remain patient.

### "The Unexpected Is Not the Impossible" "Client #4"

I adhere to a regular early morning exercise regimen at the local YMCA. Given that I have some sense of fashion as well as a strong desire for comfort, I wear fairly high-end workout clothes. Most at the gym pay at least passing attention to their gear. The notable exception over the years was a man who was much dedicated to using the equipment, putting in time and doing his reps, but who always wore fresh-from-the-field bib overalls. I spoke with him from time to time when we shared weights. Mostly we chatted about community events. Although he occasionally asked me how the market was doing, I interpreted this more as his polite attempt to give me something to comment on than as any preliminary interest in financial planning discussions. He gave every indication of being a man of modest means. My assessment/assumption was wildly incorrect.

One day he called me to make an appointment. He said, "I have a problem and I don't know what to do. I'm hoping you can help." The following day he came to my office bearing his "problem." He was carrying a retail store bag… and this contained Berkshire-Hathaway stock certificates that turned out to be worth a bit over $7 million. He'd had these for years. In conversation, Client #4 defined why he considered the bag's contents problematic: the assets were not in a form that allowed him to accomplish certain goals, to satisfy hopes, to enjoy the benefits of his wealth. It was as though he had a beautiful piece of land and all the building materials for a mansion, but no architectural plans. Client #4 was clear and plain-spoken, so it was not long before we created plans for a financial structure he could live in with great satisfaction for the rest of his life. And, no, he did not start showing up in flashy workout gear; the bib overalls remained.

I share the story of Client #4 because he is, on many levels, probably the most unexpected client of my career. But the point is that I never treated him in a manner that would have made it impossible for him to feel welcome as a client. He knew from our contacts that I was helpful, cordial, informative and sometimes entertaining. Had I been unhelpful, rude, dismissive and boring, the possibility of his becoming a client would have faded. Being open to/with others means being open to/for the unexpected. And I think that's essential to being open for business.

Now, a few words on love. "What?!" I've noted elsewhere how important it is to love what you do for work. Now I want to underscore the importance of loving people… in a way that is expansive and clearly defined.

The ancient Greeks had three words for love: eros (romantic or erotic love), philio (brotherly/sisterly/friendship love) and agape. It's agape I want to focus on. Agape (rhymes with poppy) is more an act of will than a feeling. It is centered around the notion of seeking the best for another through caring and committed actions. It is explicitly all-inclusive and non-judgmental. It is, to my mind, the most fitting way to interact with all persons… and it is foundational to building an "everyone's a potential client" business. It is principled and profoundly effective.

A friend of mine who's a baseball nut told me that my job was, "A lot like being a good infielder or outfielder." I had no idea what he was talking about. "Look," he explained, "A fielder has no idea when a ball will be hit to him but he does try to put himself in a most likely position and to be ready at all times. When the ball does come to him – that's called a 'chance' – he either does what his instincts and skills enable by fielding the ball correctly, or he flubs it – an error. You never know where or when a client will come along. You just prepare and position, then hope your instincts and skills are sharp enough so you don't flub it." This image is pretty much spot-on, and I suggest that cultivating a capacity for agape is a crucial skill to develop.

Through the years, I have practiced agape and I have fielded count-less clients. Some of the chances I've flubbed, but most I've handled well. And because I've been open to the possible/serendipitous/unexpected and keep the door of my business wide open to all, my clients include: CEO's, mill workers, a surgeon I've never met, news makers and news reporters, community business owners and first responders, elderly women who bring me cookies and elderly men who gab about local sports, newlyweds doing their first financial family planning, folks whose expertise I rely on (doctors, bankers, mechanics, trainers, etc.), people who count heavily on me (widows/widowers, persons at a loss for guidance), and, yes… a disheveled office walk-in…a TV star… a skiing executive and a lost date… and a guy working out in bib overalls.

### "Anyone Can Be a Source of Inspiration"

Any person who is not open to inspiration will expire. Physically, if we don't open our mouths/noses to take in air, our bodies will die/expire for lack of oxygen essential to life. Professionally, if we don't open our hearts/minds to new ideas made available through a myriad of relationships and sources, our business can die for lack of the input and energy necessary to sustain it. We need inspiration and, if we're alert and receptive, we will discover that we are surrounded constantly by sources that supply it.

The root meaning of "inspiration" traces back to the Latin word spirare, "to breathe into." This had a quite literal meaning of, "to give life," but it also took on the figurative and metaphysical meaning of, "to fill with spirit" (from the related Latin word spiritus). Given this etymological background, we get a clear sense that inspiration is something downright important! My goal for the next few pages is to encourage you to examine your life and career with the intent of identifying sources of inspiration… persons who have helped you gain a spirit of excitement for your life work, persons who have lifted you up when you have been dispirited, those who have offered you ideas or insights (by whatever means) that have seemed "a breath of fresh air," those whose stories or experiences have stoked your life energy. To identify our sources of inspiration leads to gratitude; to open ourselves to new sources of inspiration signifies wisdom.

There are a number of people in my life who have inspired me to be better and to do better. Several of these might be considered fairly predictable sources of positive influence... my parents, a dedicated teacher, an influential coach, an early business contact. But what I most want you to be alert for and receptive to is the "surprising inspirer." I'll share a couple of stories from my career that may help you envision how anyone can be a source of inspiration.

## #1 "The Unknown Inspirer Who Enabled My Career"

During basic and intermediate sales schools, I had won some prizes for most sales. This was initially pretty heady, but then I, like many before, hit a dry spell. The easy sales were gone and I was being confronted with more potential clients saying "no" than saying "yes." It had become discouraging, and I had decided to quit the business on a certain day after one more scheduled contact.

Just before I'd made this decision, my mother had noticed one evening that I was less interested than usual in her meatloaf. This activated her motherly instinct and she correctly intuited that something was troubling me. "What's up?" she inquired. I told her my plan and she had an immediate, firm response. "Give it one more year," she said. "If you feel the same then, I'll help you quit." I agreed.... And things turned around.

Fifteen years later, I had become quite successful in sales and as a speaker. Sadly, my mother was dying. On one of my visits to her, I made it a point to thank her for encouraging me to continue with my business. She was, at the time, in and out of lucidity, but she stated, "I wouldn't have done it except for that letter." "What letter?" I asked, not sure if she was speaking of something real or imagined. She directed me to a very real file. I pulled out the letter she referred to and read it. It affected me deeply, for it had changed the course of my life. A mentor at one of my early sales schools had written this letter to my parents. In it, he spoke highly of the ability and potential I had. My parents, I believe wisely, never mentioned this letter to me, but it had served as the impetus for my mother's sturdy encouragement.

This early mentor, through a gracious letter expressing thoughtful observation, had been my "unknown inspirer." Because he made that effort of outreach, he affected my life in a profoundly positive way. Happily, while at a speaking engagement years later, I was able to express a personal thanks to the letter writer.

Please note: The events I just recounted should remind us (they did me!) of how important it is to offer support to newcomers in our business in whatever ways seem appropriate. Since immortality is a status none of us can attain, our goal should be to do all we can to ensure the competent continuity of our business. We all benefit.

### #2 "The Chance Roommate Who Became Both Inspirer-in-Chief and Steadfast Friend"

When I first qualified to attend the Million Dollar Round Table, I had only the vaguest possible idea of what that meant. A colleague smartened me up briskly and bluntly: "Go to the meeting. It will be life-changing." Fortunately, I was willing to set aside my ignorance for that sage advice. I attended, but my roommate never showed up. The next year I was on my own as well. It had become clear that these events were professionally high-value.

The following year at a Disney World business meeting, I struck up a conversation with a colleague named Greg. We connected on our ideas about career, family, life in general. So I asked if he would be interested in rooming with me for the next Million Dollar Round Table. It would be an opportunity to share take-away ideas, critiques, learnings and strategies. He agreed.

Twenty-seven years later, I can report that we've been roommates each year. The interchange over that span of time has enriched us both. Greg had been in our business about five years more than I, so he served me early on as a mentor and a voice of experience (his father had also been in sales). But as our relationship deepened and matured, the exchange became more mutually beneficial and enlightening. Initially, Greg kept me focused and pushed me to learn as much as possible; we held two-person "study groups" during which I came to have high regard for Greg's veteran perspectives and experience-based wisdom. Over time, I was able to contribute some fresh insights and innovative takes on long-standing issues. Professionally, we developed a strong mutual admiration; personally, we bonded into an enduring friendship. It is now as comfortable to talk family events as contract specifics.

This relationship with Greg, I think it is accurate to say, has evolved into a cherished source of mutual inspiration. Whether this came about through fate or circumstance or providence or dumb luck (label it as you will!), the result has been a meaningful bond and a prime example of how "anyone can be a source of inspiration." Cultivate the options/opportunities for such relationships in your life.

These two stories provide instances of inspiring connections. Both centered around individuals with whom I'd had personal contact. But face-to-face contact is a limited realm. The good news is that our resources for inspiration are vastly larger… more extensive… virtually unlimited. Setting aside the assets available via Internet access and selected social media, I want to note that reading – tapping into the insights, imaginings, experiences and understandings of others – is your basic means of finding intellectual stimulation and nutrition. Reading piques your curiosity and feeds your mind. I'm not saying anything here that thousands of others (teachers, parents, media figures, etc.) haven't said, but I do want to be clear about the reason I'm advocating for reading. Bluntly stated, reading is an antidote to laziness. There's a place in our lives for settling back into a somewhat passive "entertain me" mode, but reading has the implicit hook of "engage me."

Through my youth, I had never been a great reader, but early in my career I met a fellow who invited me to work with him. Tragically, he died in an accident, but he left me a massively consequential legacy gift. He gave me copies of The Feldman Method and Creative Selling by Ben Feldman, and reading these, digesting their wisdom, gave me a hunger for reading. I got turned on to books. (With this book, I hope to inspire your appetite for more!) The next ignition point to fire my desire for reading came when I read High Touch Selling by John Savage and had the opportunity to meet him.

He has a wonderful way of expressing his desire to have people always in the learning mode. He charges people to "stay green," to lean towards growth and never to turn towards the brown/decay of accepted/aging/unchanged ideas. The writer Eudora Welty once penned a memorable line about the growth of spring: "Nature's first green is gold." For persons in sales, staying "green" is the path to achieving "gold."

Over time, lovers of reading have encouraged people to develop a "catholicity of tastes" that pushes us in an entirely healthy direction… towards reading materials that strengthen us intellectually just as an eclectic mix of vitamins, minerals and exercise contributes to our physical health. The benefits of wide-ranging reading cannot be strictly categorized, but I'll set before you a few of the lessons I derive from the array of genres I enjoy…. Reading history gives me a feel for the long view of things and for the way key decisions have ripple-effect impacts over time. Reading biographies (especially of politicians, athletes, entertainers and corporate leaders) often informs me about how adversity is confronted and overcome, about how principles guide performance. Fiction engages me in the nuances of human behavior and helps me understand the plot twists of real life.

In putting together this chapter that incorporates my core beliefs that, "anyone is a potential client," and, "anyone can be a source of inspiration," I realized that bringing these beliefs to tangible fruition demanded one more thing. So, mark this….

If I were to choose one word to describe the ideal stance/status/position of a person in sales, it would be receptivity. This is the "activator trait" for sales persons, something we need to develop in a joyfully dedicated manner. Yes, it's fun. Yes, it's crucial. I've already noted the importance of being receptive to potential clients who range from the "outrageous outlier" to the "unreachable star." But the deeper impact of receptivity has to do with an internal attitude towards learning. One of the most profound insights I've ever had about how to approach my work is one that has also led to a deeper level of calmness and satisfaction. This insight expresses itself in a daily personal goal: I make it my intent to learn something new. Notice that I'm not saying: I make it my intent to make a sale. By focusing on the process of learning and not the endgame of sales, I make sure that I'm equipping myself to become more proficient in my work and more knowledgeable about my world. The sales will come. To trust that this will be the case is enormously freeing, and it is really the practical application of John Savage's wise "stay green" advice.

You will, by the way, discover that when you become receptive to learning something or many things new every day, the sources for that learning are unlimited. I've mentioned reading as a primary source, but useful wisdom is all around us… in the comment of a child, in passing conversation with a colleague, in a news report, in a daydream, in a newspaper cartoon. When we make ourselves receptive, when we commit to opening our minds, we gain a valuable understanding of how, wondrously, everyone can be a source of inspiration.

I hope that the stories and insights I've shared in this chapter have been both entertaining and encouraging. If they help you to consider ways you can become more "open" as a person -- more open to surprise and opportunity, more open-hearted and open-minded – that's a positive! I do know that I have grown away from fairly narrow views on client possibilities and from rather limited understandings about sources of inspiration. I'm grateful that I chose to change, and I truly believe that if I can do it, you can, too!

# 9. "Investing in Dividends Pays People…. Investing in People Pays Dividends"

It is likely that you expected me, at some point, to write about investments. I'm about to do that. What may be a bit of a surprise (or disappointment!) is that I will not be presenting you with hot, can't-miss, innovative materials about strategies, schemes, sectors and statistical models. What I offer instead is effective, simple, straightforward… and absolutely essential. Beyond one brief but important example, I leave it to others to tell you how to invest in products; my focus is on how to invest in people.

The core principles covered in this chapter originated in my understanding of and appreciation for the merits of a particular type of investment. DRIPs. Early on in my career as an investment advisor, I realized that dividend reinvestment programs (DRIPs) could be – and often <u>needed</u> to be – a major component of a client's long-term financial plan. DRIPs do a number of valuable things, among them:

A. They encourage establishing a pattern of regular scheduled investment;

B. They invite spontaneous additional investment (most plans welcome occasional additions of $50.00 or more);

C. They reduce the non-productive and ultimately futile attempt to time the markets;

D. They can produce a rather reliable income stream in the future;

E. They set in place, through quarterly reinvestment of dividend income, an automatic savings plan;

F. They tend to lower the anxiety level and to reward the steadfastness of investors;

G. They guide people toward solid companies with long dividend-paying histories;

H. They provide superb generational gifts to heirs.

It became clear to me that, "investing dividends pays people." Many clients have benefited from this basic understanding.

What I suggest to you is that we extrapolate from that understanding, that we extend its message, that we commit in our business lives to the belief that "investing in people pays dividends."

Our general use of the word "investment" is to designate something of value, specifically something that we believe can increase in value. It was in my family that I first got a sense of how to apply that word to people. I was fortunate, and for that I am grateful. Though my family had modest material means, they possessed one priceless asset – the commitment to invest in me. That investment took form in providing me with love and acceptance, in giving me a strong work ethic, in passing along to me a wealth of wisdom about right and wrong and the necessity of time off, in being tenacious about addressing my vision issues. In my case, a sense of self-worth and personal value grew out of parental investment in me. All of us, I believe, have persons in our lives who fulfill this mentoring role, who invest something of themselves because they value us and hope to see us grow.

The gracious response to a kindness extended is to pass it along to others. I try to do this with my own children…. By creating opportunities for travel and for seeing/experiencing new things together. By helping them discern and define life-options. By having special days. By letting them know that my own work is in part for them. By trying to understand their struggles.

By sharing beliefs and events. By acknowledging higher meaning or spiritual power. By having family dinners. I am certainly not infallible in doing these things, but I am intentional. And that intention has moved me to act in a manner that builds upon the ways my parents invested in me.

I offer the preceding two paragraphs not to be nostalgic or hokey, and I also recognize that many have experienced a very different upbringing from the positive one I've described. But whatever your history, whatever your current relational situation or standing, my message remains heartfelt and consistent: invest yourself in those you care about and act upon the intention of somehow making their lives better. From a practical point of view, our industry is absolutely dependent upon people's desire to do precisely what I advocate! Consider… Why would anyone buy life insurance if he/she did not see it as making a positive investment in the future of a valued person?

Before giving some thoughts on key people in our business lives, I want to note the origins of the word "investment." It comes from the Latin investio, meaning "to clothe, to cover, to surround." I suspect that when most of us get dressed for an event or activity, we pay a bit of attention to what we put on. We want our clothes to be comfortable, to be durable, to be suited for the task at hand. In our business, the people we surround ourselves with, the staff we "put on" payroll, should have similar attributes. They should be personable (comfortable to work with), reliable (durable) and competent (able to handle the tasks at hand). These are the things we need to look for when we invest in persons. And, just as the clothes we wear can be a form of self-expression, those we hire should be able to convey to clients our own thoughts and values.

Well-considered investment in DRIPs can provide a basis for financial success, and wise investment in the persons who comprise your staff can foster business success. I offer a half-dozen pieces of advice for you to ponder as you make the personnel investments that can bear countless dividends.

1. Hire sooner than later. My first hired staff person was brought on to address anticipated need, not to meet needs currently apparent. It was one of the wisest moves I ever made, though I had to swallow hard on the financial commitment it entailed (paying someone else before

paying myself!). What I learned from this experience, and what I pass on to you, is that just as any financial investment involves risk, so does any investment in a person. But what I purchased with my investment was <u>time</u>. The dividends I received were the opportunities to explore what I could do best, the capacity to discern and determine where I would allocate my energy. Acting upon anticipated need is far more beneficial than reacting to overwhelming current ones.

2. Don't hire clones of yourself. By stating that, I mean this: add people to your staff whose skills complement yours rather than duplicating them. Honestly assess what you do well, what you enjoy and need little help on, and then hire people who can do other needed tasks better. Doing this is both an exercise in humility and an exercise in business savvy. The financial equivalent would be this… we know that it is almost never smart to put all resources or hopes in one sector. Diversification is prudent both in portfolio and personnel decisions. Creating a broad base of skills within the office setting is as wise as creating a divergent set of investment assets. Amplify the capability of your business by adding a wide range of talents/skills/areas of expertise. The analogy of a sports teams is applicable, too. When putting together a team, management seeks out players with skills suited to particular positions and then works to blend them into a cohesive, high-functioning unit. A soccer team comprised solely of defenders would likely have a tough time scoring enough goals; a baseball team made up entirely of pitchers would be laughable. Winning in athletic endeavors takes a well-selected roster featuring a range of needed skills; creating a winning office staff requires the same.

3. Recognize that expansion has expenses. If you hire the right person for a job, be prepared to pay a bit more than the prevailing wage for the position. Paying the "going rate" may mean just that… a qualified, desirable employee may end up going elsewhere. Whenever possible, seek first to increase an employee's hours (mutually beneficial) and then increase pay and responsibilities. In that order. As more money comes into your business, share with others who have helped make

that happen. This is the form of dividend reinvestment on a practical, personal level.

4. Delegate tasks. The earlier you determine what tasks you can delegate to others with confidence in the outcome, the better for your business, your personal well-being, your potential for expansion. The practice of delegation breaks you free from any tendencies toward micro-management, tendencies that almost always impinge upon business success. In relation to your business and its ultimate direction, it is better to adopt the role of visionary and manager than that of someone who does day-to-day tasks or deals with ordinary operations. Your role/goal is to: provide necessary training for those you hire, assess how the work is getting done, give feedback and guidance... then, let go! Ceding to others the tasks that sap energy/time is a huge net gain to you.

5. Outsource what seems appropriate. Sometimes it may be possible to outsource tasks that are repetitive or massive or that do not require the full capabilities of your staff. Putting these things in the hands of others can prove both efficient and cost-effective... and may even improve morale. At other times, testing or pursuing a new goal may require outsourcing, especially if staff time is maximized serving clients. For example, I found it wise to hire a marketing firm one day a week to assist with advertising, to prospect new clients and revenue streams. My investment in their work allowed me to assess my options/opportunities without taking staff time and attention away from valued current clients.

6. Take care in hiring staff and extend care for them when they are on board. Just as you take care in choosing the DRIP stocks that will comprise a portfolio (quality counts!), your investment in those with whom you interact daily requires similar care. When chosen carefully, both investments will grow in value long-term.

If you are careful in hiring, it follows that you should be caring toward those you welcome into your business. Our ways of expressing that caring will be based upon our personal styles and preferences and levels of creativity, but there are some basic categories that should, I believe, be addressed through our words and actions. These are the areas in which I conduct my forays (4 A's) into staff support:

A-1: Attention – Pay attention to staff needs… everything from necessary updating of equipment to a bit of extra time off.

A-2: Affirmation – Note, compliment and affirm work that exceeds expectations.

A-3: Acknowledgement – Point out regularly that success is a team effort and that staff interaction with clients is the primary face of the business.

A-4: Acceptance – Accept your own responsibility as a leader. This means showing that you are working intently on making the business thrive, recognizing that mistakes by staff are things you own as well, offering your time for listening to ideas and concerns. In short, show that you are engaged, accessible and appreciative. I have always believed that it is crucial for staff to respect me as well as to know that I care for/about them; 4-A is foundational to building respect.

In the realm of food, bread is known as the "staff of life." In the realm of business, your staff is your staff of life. It is they who provide the sustenance for your business… and for you.

Elsewhere in this book, I refer to my business motto: "It's not about me; it's about them." These words serve as an ingrained reminder that I am, in the best possible sense, a servant whose goal is to meet the needs of others. That given, the emphasis of the next portion of this chapter becomes understandable and noteworthy. It focuses on investing in oneself. Bottom line, the more competent I become, the more I can perceive and address my clients' needs and goals, the better an investment I become to them. My efforts at self-improvement and skills enhancement pay dividends to clients. And the more value I bring to my clients, the better for business.

There are numerous ways we can invest in ourselves that will bring this greater value to clients. Some skill-sharpening is targeted at handling specific situations or niche products. Some enhancements of abilities emerge organically from our particular business context and practices. Some growth opportunities are completely serendipitous and others are meticulously planned.

Every person entering our industry is a potential gem of great value to clients. But we also enter the field as rough gemstones unshaped by the experience that will enable us to begin to shine. Experience provides us with occasions and opportunities that are "cutting edge" in the sense that they give new facets to our careers... new abilities, insights, perspectives. And as a multi-faceted gem gains brilliance and value, a multi-faceted person in our industry also tends to shine forth and to become invaluable to clients.

The suggestions I offer below may not all strike you as "cutting edge," but they all identify opportunities for you to be shaped, to become more polished, to take on new angles of understanding, to gain enlightenment, to increase both your sense of self-worth and your value to clients. I recommend them all as wise investments in yourself.

Invest yourself in education. It is, of course, a professional obligation to keep up on the broad issues of our business – regulations, products, ethical standards, etc. But there are so many available options that can help us become more multi-faceted in our knowledge. These include such things as seminars, continuing education, presentations at industry functions, college/higher education courses. Do research to find out which ones are truly high quality.

There is a small town in Wales whose name is Llanfairpwllgwyngyllgogerychwyr-drobwlllllantysiliogogogoch. Residents are quite proud of having a town designated by more letters than any other place in the world. In our profession it can be seductive to add a string of letters after our names to signify certain levels of achievement. My experience with clients is that such an alphabet soup presentation is often more off-putting and confusing than helpful. It can seem pretentious and designed to turn conversation to be about you. My advice: list those letters that mean the most to you in terms of achieving wisdom and skills that are client-beneficial.

Invest yourself in giving dinner seminars. Such events require cash investment, but they allow you to be a gracious host, to convey carefully selected information that you believe helpful, to listen to the concerns and issues of those who are your guests, to describe the scope of your services, to invite further conversation, to thank persons who attend. These events are an investment in building a reputation. They provide the groundwork for harvesting future inquiries generated by the informational seeds you plant.

Invest yourself in teaching. At the most basic level, teaching involves challenging ourselves to "know our stuff," to devise ways of presenting material in an attention-holding manner, to be ready for questions and push-back. What I'm saying is that self-learning and thorough preparation are the precursors to teaching others. This is great discipline for all future contacts with clients! Taking the opportunity to teach, whether in a short seminar or an extended course, also identifies you as someone with expertise, as someone through whom persons can gain access to needed information. As we know, it is unethical to "go after" students as clients, so teaching serves a healthy function in allowing us to interact with people as people, not as potential transactions. It has been my experience, however, that students do refer others to me…. "He taught me a lot and gave some valuable insights. Give him a try."

Invest yourself in sending traditional mailings. "OK," you're saying to yourself, "Who let this dinosaur into the room?" Yes, dinosaurs are extinct, but the human capacity to respond to personal contact is alive and well. In an environment where we are besieged by targeted ads, algorithmically generated data and social media trivia, a hand-written mailing can have tremendous impact. Let me ask again, as I did in my comments about thank you notes… If, in the stack of mail you receive, there is a hand-written letter, would you not be inclined to open it first or to regard it as something special? Making the effort to do such personal messaging conveys that we "have time" for the needs and concerns of the recipient. Certainly and effectively, the majority of our client contacts will be via emails, texts and mass-produced materials. But don't ignore the value of investing, at selected times, in traditional personal correspondence.

Invest yourself in the tasks of analyst/biographer/documentary-maker/ sleuth. What on earth does this mean?! It's my way of advising and encouraging you to be curious about your clients. An analyst strives to know how a person thinks. A biographer attempts to understand a person's life-story in as complete a way as possible. A documentary-maker focuses on events that had great impact. A sleuth seeks out pertinent details and clues about persons and events. In no way am I suggesting that you be prying. Being invasive into a client's life is neither welcome nor proper. What I am advocating is that you be perceptive, receptive and alert when it comes to learning about your clients. Wise decisions about stock-picking emerge only from a process of due diligence, of asking plenty of questions about the workings of a company. Making wise decisions about how best to meet a client's needs means getting a real feel for that person's inner workings. I think of it as caring curiosity. The easiest way to practice it is to maintain a consistently fresh set of questions that will help you better understand your client. For example: What are their feelings about family? How do they feel about their work situation? What are their relational needs and necessities? What are their best-loved activities? What are some of their volunteer involvements and favorite non-profits? What are their patterns of behavior and ways of approaching issues? What do they feel about solitude and community? How do they respond to humor? You get the idea! The possible questions are endless and I urge you to keep a list that evolves as your relationship extends over time. To understand your clients better is to bring greater value to your service.

Invest yourself in the goal of personal growth. I speak to this in a variety of ways in other portions of this book, but here I want to underscore the investment value of you as the most important business asset. One of the most wonderful aspects of being human is that we have the capacity to learn from our cumulative life experiences. I am grateful daily that I don't have the same behaviors or outlooks or levels of knowledge that I did as a child or teenager. What's especially exciting is that in our adult lives we can be quite intentional about how we use what we learn. We can, in very tangible ways, choose the kind of person we want to be. Whatever our experiences, resources or circumstances, we can always try to set ourselves on a course of positive maturation. Sounds trite, but there's a deep truth: It's worth the effort to try becoming a better person. More engaging… more trustworthy… more personable… more knowledgeable. This has obvious business implications. Given the choice between someone who is competent but boring and someone who is competent and interesting, most clients will select the latter. Ideally, my clients will enjoy being around me, and one of the finest compliments (and advertisements!) I can get is to have a client say to another person: "You should check out Scott. He's an interesting guy and he's done a great job for me." I'll be saying more about possible components of "personal diversification" in the eleventh chapter. For now, suffice it to say that investing in yourself pays dividends in enhancing the quality of your relationships with others.

The results of our ability to invest in financial products usually get revealed in year-end summaries and long-term income streams. The results of our ability to invest in people take more subtle forms such as office efficiency, client satisfaction and loyalty, and personal contentment. These things are less chartable than numerical data, but they are probably more crucial to the bottom-line success of our business. I hope that in this chapter I've encouraged you to shape and sharpen the people-investing skills I've outlined. It takes intention and commitment, but surely, **if I can do it, you can, too!**

# 10. "Essentials"

Throughout this book, I've provided you with suggestions, ideas, techniques and approaches that can help you attain success in your business and personal life. From all this material, you can select the pieces that best suit your own goals and strengths and style. You have choices to make. <u>But</u>… there are some things that are not optional. They are essential. They are the <u>sine qua non</u> factors for achieving success, and they are the focus of this chapter.

In just about every area of life we can recognize the importance of those things deemed essential. In relationships, we identify those qualities we consider essential to forming an enduring bond. In recipes or pharmaceuticals, there are essential ingredients that make a dish tasty and nutritious, that make a drug therapeutically effective. In business settings there are certain people considered essential employees, those without whom work would cease, falter or fail. In novels and movies, it is essential that there be a plot in order to hold audience interest. In planning a hike, one needs to distinguish between the essentials and the extraneous so that our backpack does not get impossibly heavy. I could give lots more examples… but that's not essential. To the point, what <u>is</u> absolutely crucial for persons in our industry is that we understand the essentials that pertain to success in our business careers.

Do you know the origin of the word "essential"? It's revealing! It comes from the Latin <u>esse</u>, meaning, "to be." That implies that <u>who we are</u> is of primary importance. Specifically, in the business context, who I am in relation to staff and clients – the people with whom I have the most contact – needs to draw my greatest attention.

So what I offer you is not a "to do" list but rather a "to be" list. And I'll identify some actions that, for me, seem essential ways of translating being into doing.

## With Clients:

Be present. Initially – and ongoing – this means prospecting. It is quite obvious that you cannot be present to clients if you have none. This is an unending task, one in which you will use some of the same kinds of tools used by those who prospect for minerals. Identification of target. Research. Acquisition of necessary equipment. Strategy for access. Investment of time and effort. As you become more practiced in prospecting, you will come to identify the kinds of clients you work best with, the ways of finding and reaching them, the level of personal energy it will take to serve them well. Prospecting is unceasing but rewarding. And you will become more adept the more you do.

Being present also implies advertising/visibility. For decades, I have made my presence known in the community through consistent ongoing ads at a local movie theater and in an area newspaper. Through them, I get people to note again and again, "There's Scott!" By being present in this way I make it more likely that they will be in touch with me in a time of need.

Being present to clients long-term means attentiveness and contact. I've stated this and provided examples elsewhere in the book. Restating it now simply underscores its importance.

Be efficient. In initial conversations with clients, my number one goal is to determine the focal point at which desire, need and financial capacity come together. This defines the result that my client and I can work together to produce. I ask lots of questions and listen more than talk. Key among the questions are ones that clearly identify a client's risk tolerance; without knowing this, I put myself at risk of devising a financial plan that my client would find unacceptable or emotionally unsettling. So I try to discern if any of their leisure activities involve a degree of risk. And I ask, "Which would be a bigger concern for you: Having the market go up by 20% but your portfolio by 12%, or experiencing a major market event and having your portfolio shrink by half its value?" And I inquire, "Are you here more because you want to be rich or more because you want to avoid being poor?" Agreeing on a level of risk tolerance is essential to working productively/effectively with a client.

Being efficient also requires setting in place a solid communication system with a client. This is generally remarkably simple to establish and serves to eliminate mixed/missed messages, timeliness issues and accessibility snafus. The question to get answered is: "What communication medium do you prefer, check regularly and respond to reliably?" Giving a client the opportunity to make this choice demonstrates that you want to keep close contact and to respect their preferences. For urgent matters that may require a phone call, it is important to know the best number for access and the names of any people with whom you can leave information.

Your level of efficiency will also rise when, in contacts with carriers, you determine who the key people are in terms of getting things done. You will almost always learn who these individuals are not by studying the carrier's job designations or organizational chart, but rather through numerous interactions. Experience is the teacher here. Make note of who can facilitate transactions, who expedites paperwork, who has the best knowledge of products, who deals calmly with special situations, who understands the carrier's history and structure. Being efficient means recognizing these people and cultivating your relationship with them. Make yourself someone they want to assist.

Be creative. Clients quickly and rightly get put off if they feel that you have one product (or set of products) to sell and that your energy is going into convincing them to buy it. If that is in any way your approach, abandon it. Your energy should go into being creative. The difference is as great as between selling a prefab house or designing a custom home, as between selling a car off the lot or ordering one with all the desired accessories.

In our conversations with clients, we take the time to ask wide-ranging questions in order to get a clear picture of need and as a way of truly coming to know the persons we serve. I like to think of the initial ingathering of information as a process very similar to what a suit- or dress-maker does when measuring someone for custom attire. The measurements must be accurate.

They must take into account all the individual nuances of size and shape. The suit- or dress-maker must be creative in using the data gathered, for he or she knows that when it comes to an article of fine clothing, there is no such thing as "one size fits all." So, too, we need to be creative in constructing a financial plan from the information we have obtained, for there is no "one size fits all" in our realm as well. Our task is to "tailor" a group of products for our clients, to use our knowledge and insights to piece together something that truly fits.

Most suit- or dress-makers know something important… they know that what they are selling is not just a product comprised of silk or wool or such. If they use their skills and creativity to the highest level, their clients will receive something greater as a product – the experience of comfort, the feeling of being tended to, the assurance of looking good. Similarly, we need to be aware that what we are selling is not just a collection of policies and portfolio pieces. If we use our expertise and creativity to the best of our capability, our clients get something of incalculable value – the experience of knowing that their concerns and needs have been suitably addressed, the feeling of assurance that things are in place.

Be humble. I have not forgotten that I've already devoted a chapter to humility, but I want to stress one particular aspect that merits being tagged as essential. This: Being humble requires that we apologize to clients when we make mistakes. Oversights. Missed deadlines. Faulty figures. Inattention. The possibilities in our precise yet complex business are innumerable, and no matter what level of precautionary care we maintain, we will make some mistakes. Being human means being fallible.

And being humble allows us to respond to our mistakes in ways that are personally positive and relationally restorative. To apologize for an error is in fact an illustration of ethical strength. It conveys to a client that you are self-aware and self-monitoring, that you possess the integrity to commu-nicate in a completely honest and forthright manner. It also provides the opportunity to assure a client that you will make amends. Your apology is not "just words;" it implies corrective action and affirms that it's important to note this. "I'm sorry. I can make mistakes, but I'll fix it. Please give me the chance to do so." No matter what the cause of the mistake – bad information, staff miscues, bureaucratic confusion, regrettable negligence – your apology should never place blame but rather always take responsibility with the stated commitment to setting things right.

There is no formula for apologies. They simply need to be direct and heartfelt. I use a personal note or a conversation. And I will sometimes send a small gift (a consumable or flowers are my preferences… they indicate caring but go away over time as the mistake gets addressed). You will discover what best allows you to deliver a sincere apology.

Yes, being human means we make mistakes. Being humble gives us the courage to admit them, learn from them and put into action a helpful response.

Be grateful. I'll reiterate the obvious: no clients, no business. Every day, I feel grateful that people place their trust in me to help them achieve important life goals. This gratitude is not something I should keep to myself. Regularly and with dedication, I let my clients know through various means of contact that I appreciate their confidence in my ability to assist them. My fervent belief is that we cannot thank our clients too much. If the key to improving athletic skills and teamwork is, "practice, practice, practice;" the key to establishing outstanding client relations is, "thank you, thank you, thank you."

### With Staff:

Be positive. The workplace is filled with chores, tasks, demands and client demands that are sometimes challenging. Members of your staff will count on you to have a we-can-do-it attitude and to have skill at anticipating needs or concerns. Such an attitude and such a skill-set are marks of positive leadership. So ask two questions: 1) Do we have in place great people, clear office procedures and the best equipment for handling the tasks at hand? 2) Am I always trying to stay one step ahead in all matters concerning the business? If you can answer these questions affirmatively, you can confidently be positive toward staff in your leadership role.

Being positive with staff also means, I believe, creating what I call "structural affirmations." These include such things as a bonus system, flexibility of scheduling when possible, a comfortable and warm and safe work environment, good pay, means of acknowledging special efforts or notable occasions. My additional advice in relation to building a positive esprit de corps is to let all reprimands be expressed in private and all accolades be celebrated together. Concerns require confidentiality; achievement needs applause!

Be direct. In dealing with staff, it is essential that you give clear tasks and time frames. Anything along the lines of, "I think I want something like this…" is imprecise and unacceptable. It is up to us to describe the elements and scope of a job. This means naming the what/when/why/for whom elements of a job and stating the form of the end product. This process allows for self-clarification and invites questions. Staff will appreciate this. As a check to see if my intent and messages are clear, I invite staff to repeat back my instructions. This minimizes misunderstandings.

Be responsive. If you have hired well, that is, brought into your office people with initiative, intelligence and skills complementary to yours, you need to maintain an open professional dialogue. In the course of their work, staff will likely come up with ideas for enhancing the operation of the business. Let it be known that your ears are receptive to innovative thoughts. Staff meetings or private conversations can provide the venue. I want to note that not every suggestion will be implemented (though you can honestly affirm that all are welcome). You should evolve over time a mutual understanding with staff about the "I-know-best areas" and the "You-may-know-best areas." This is a kind of role-clarification that can be nothing but beneficial. It, coupled with your attitude of empowering openness, will build a respect for whatever decisions you make about adopting or not adopting suggestions.

Being responsive also means paying attention to nitty-gritty in-office needs. When staff expresses concerns about equipment, vendor contacts, communication systems, etc., do tend to the issue promptly. It is far better to have staff feeling, "I'm being heard," than, "He/she doesn't care." Your responsiveness indicates that you value the work being done in the office. It is a key component to keeping a high level of staff morale… and to keeping staff.

[A brief aside…. Staff stability is a treasure of inestimable value. Turnover is costly in multiple negative ways. It inhibits a consistent flow of business growth. It saps your energy. It draws on your time for retraining. It conveys a sense of organizational instability to clients. Once you have good staff in place, it pays to develop your "response-abilities" in order to retain them.]

Be humble. What! Again? Yes, again. I bring it up in order to state the importance of recognizing that in relation to staff, although you are the boss, you are also a co-worker. And just as you appreciate their apologies for mistakes made, they appreciate yours. I maintain that it is all-around healthy to have "office ownership" of mistakes… if all deal with the consequences, all can pitch in to rectify and make amends. Your leadership in setting this policy and your adherence to it contribute greatly to building staff respect for your leadership, to providing reason for loyalty.

To be humble within the office environment also means that during times when tasks seem overwhelming or when interruptions have impaired staff's ability to keep on schedule, you convey your willingness to pitch in. Helping do things that are in the staff's job-description (assuming you can!) makes a deeply meaningful statement. It affirms that you are not, as a person, "above" them; you are "with" them. The difference between those two prepositions (above vs. with) is huge. "Above" implies an attitude that is hierarchical and arrogant; "with" is collaborative and humble. And, by sharing tasks together for the mutual benefit of the business, you may just have some fun.

A wrap-up. My presenting you with what I identify as essentials does not in any way prescribe a set or regimented course of action. I'm simply providing you with the raw materials, the resources, for you to build a successful business.

To make my point and purpose clear, let's consider these examples…. The alphabet or a set of characters can be considered the essentials for creating poems, stories, articles, novels – vast varieties of texts. And a limited number of notes or tones can be considered the essentials for composing jingles, songs, symphonies, operas – every musical piece in the world. The essentials I've set before you in this chapter are like the alphabet/characters or the notes/tones. There are countless ways to use them, but you are the author or composer who can turn them into something meaningful and deeply satisfying, something that will have a strong positive impact on your business.

This chapter is more about being than doing. Over time, I have chosen to strive to be present, efficient, creative, grateful, positive, direct, responsive, humble. That's the personal story I want to write with my days, the tune that is my life-song. Now, essentially, the choice is yours to make about how you can be your best in business and beyond. Over years of maturing as a person, I have made many decisive and carefully considered choices about who I want to be as an individual and how I want to be viewed by others with whom I interact. Choosing well is a key life-challenge to be met, but if I can do it, you can, too.

# 11. "Get Out of Your Comfort Zones!"

In the preceding chapter, I offered what I tagged as the "essentials." Taken together, the contents laid out the marching orders for moving forward with your business goals. It's as though I wrote the chapter with a broad permanent marker! That would have been appropriate, for these items are in fact central to success. This chapter deals with what might be considered "peripherals." And my way of presenting them has less the character of an order than it has the tone of a suggestion that you come along on an adventure. It is, however, an adventure that will take courage and commitment.

You can treat the following pages as my heartfelt invitation for you to explore an approach to life that may become central in helping you achieve a more holistic understanding of success and accomplishment. If I could have hand-written this invitation to every reader, I would have done so, for it presents portions of my own personal decision-making journey and it beckons you to make bold personal choices about attitudes, approaches and actions.

The gist of my message is this gentle but fervent exhortation: "Get out of your comfort zones!"

Most of us have been, on various occasions, in the position of comforting someone through times of grief, illness or trying situations. This usually means helping a person move from difficult to improved circumstances… grief to acceptance, illness to healing, jarring uncertainty to satisfying stability. Our provision of comfort takes an investment of ourselves in terms of energy, effort and compassion. Comforting, as signified by its original meaning of, "encouraging or offering strength," describes a process that fully engages us.

The dynamism inherent in the act of comforting someone else is something we can lose, however, when we identify being comfortable as a state of being or a style of life that we choose for ourselves. I maintain that this is neither healthy nor growth-inducing. Just a few thoughts…. We can fill our living environment with creature comforts but find that these do not sustain happiness. We can surround ourselves with comfortable friends but discover that these relationships lack depth. We can chow down on comfort foods that conjure up warm memories but realize that they do not fulfill our full nutritional needs. We can settle into comfortable views and opinions but fail to adapt to the realities of new input. We can aspire to roll through life on a chosen comfort level but not recognize that it is the variations, the ups and downs, that enliven our journey. We can dwell in a web of self-made comfort zones… but does that inspire us to expand our minds and claim our dreams?

Stated bluntly: a comfort zone can be a cage. When we build it and inhabit it, it binds us in and inhibits our growth. Strictly remaining in a comfort zone can lead us to become lazy, unmotivated and inert. I contend that living to "create comfort" is, intrinsically, personally limiting; deciding to "choose challenge" leads in a more satisfying direction. Growth, by definition, means moving into places we have not been before.

Growth requires change (of habits, understandings, knowledge base, behaviors, goals, etc.), and change is ultimately unsettling. But in a good way! A young woman with superb business instincts and an outstanding educational foundation told a friend of mine that although she already held a solid, promising job position in her early twenties, she aspired to more. She made a memorable comment: "I can live in my comfort zone, but I might just die in it. I'm energized by change. Yes, change is scary. **But, it's OK to fear change as long as you try to change anyway.**" This is – no doubt – the attitude of a person who will achieve success.

"Getting out of your comfort zones" is not a concept that fits any tight definition, so I want to give you illustrations of three ways you might incorporate it into your life. I believe that the lessons these illustrations provide are broadly and usefully applicable….

- Getting out of your comfort zone: **linear progress**

- Getting out of your comfort zone: **a sharp turn**

- Getting out of your comfort zone: **paths of exploration**

## Linear Progress

We often speak of having a career course, a path we follow over the years. There is nothing wrong with that unless you follow it mindlessly or see it as somehow inevitable. We need to remind ourselves constantly that initiative is more important and potent than inertia. The sooner we understand that we ourselves determine how to navigate our way ahead, the better.

## My personal story provides a case in point.

I was working at a transport company and doing reasonably well for a twenty-something. On the side, I bartended. This provided a fairly comfortable existence. (Yes, I was "existing" but not thriving.) When I saw a blind ad put out by a financial services office, I responded. This was a bit of a knee-jerk, impulsive reaction that already put me outside my comfort zone of well-considered and more deliberate decisions. The person who got back to me provided some materials and sent me off in a direction I'd never before considered. "Go on twenty calls," he said, "And if you don't make more than you ever have, you can leave. If you do, you owe me one year." I liked the challenge of that and made the goal on my eighteenth call.

OK. Now I was thoroughly outside my comfort zone. I possessed one suit, a box-top desk, one phone. Perhaps serendipitously, an acquaintance in the business who was ill provided me with his business book of six hundred contacts. He wanted to keep renewals but gave me access to the other names. This enabled a small but significant step forward. It was not comfortable to pursue all these contacts as a newbie in the business, but I did. Every one.

After achieving a level of some success, it was tempting to settle in right there. My father, to his credit, pushed me. My comfort zone was emphatically that of being a solo operator, but my father noted correctly that a human voice other than mine was needed in order to make my operation a true business.

So I hired my first office staff person. The form my growth took as I stepped outside a long-established comfort zone was this: I was able to exchange the notions of, "I'm in charge," and, "I'm in control," for the more productive approaches of, "We can deal with this," and, "We can make it happen."

With competent office staff in place, I could push ahead over time through the sequential comfort zones created by obtaining professional certifications. Each level of expertise opened new challenges, but I could follow a linear progression/pathway that exists for everyone in our business. Step out of the comfort zone of acquiring one level of certification and you will be rewarded; move on to the next and your rewards will likely increase. Progress begets progress. My own path led to advancement and expanded opportunities. In brief…

I went from life underwriters' training courses to obtaining credits for certified life underwriter, then to attaining classification as CLU and RHU (registered health underwriter). I became a member of the Million Dollar Round Table quite quickly (1992) and established my own business, Investor's Choice, in 1998. That year – a momentous one – my son was born and I achieved my certification as a ChFC (chartered financial consultant). My comfort zone then might have been defined as, "stable income and predictable investments of time and effort," but a move outside that zone gave me options that benefited both me in my business and my family in its security. The road also opened to speaking engagements, travel and an increasingly diverse range of client contacts.

I am grateful that I chose to push beyond the comfort zone of limited experience, expertise and expectations. Each step forward took a degree of courage to overcome those, "what-if-I-fail" or "maybe-it's-not-worth-it" feelings, but really, the need was more for commitment than courage. I describe the actions I took as "linear progress." They are completely available to everyone in our business and they simply require the determination to keep putting one foot in front of the other. The key is **to decide** to take each step forward out of your comfort zone into a new territory of opportunity. That decision is the seed of growth.

## Sharp Turn

Whatever your opinions of the current political scene, the calling of work as a public servant is one of honor and purpose. At a very young age, I had the positive experience of knowing some deft politicians who were principled, hard-working, bright, innovative, and affirmative in seeking alliances. Their work impressed me and, I confess, a deep interest in politics got into my blood. Through my business speaking engagements, I came to realize that my words definitely had an impact on people, and I recognized how my years of listening carefully to expressed needs generated a strong capacity for empathy. So some thoughts arose: Could I use my client skills to serve constituents? Could I make the kind of positive social impact I had witnessed others doing in my youth? I had at one time served as the youngest elected local official in my state, but other than that I had devoted myself to career, family and volunteering. My business was thriving and expanding; it was providing me with a solid and profitable professional comfort zone.

The old iconic British television show Monty Python's Flying Circus used to segue from one whacky comedy sketch to another with the phrase, "And now for something completely different." That phrase aptly describes my decision of one decade ago to run for a significant statewide political position. This transition from going to the office and contacting clients to hitting the campaign trail and seeking votes was, in a word, huge. In terms of my life-journey, I label it a "sharp turn" that took me widely outside my then-existing comfort zone. I found my new course exhilarating and exhausting, uplifting and unsettling, inspiring and intrusive, collegial and contentious. I experienced a whirlwind of events and gust of feelings. Although, ultimately, I felt a degree of disillusionment (material for another book, perhaps!), I am supremely grateful that I made that sharp turn that took me decisively outside my comfort zone.

I learned so much. Yes, about our political system, but much more about myself and my business. These were things I would not have been as aware of, or aware of at all, if I had remained in my comfort zone. The insights I gained, some noted briefly earlier in this book, have proved immensely beneficial. To reiterate and to state anew, these are key positive gains from my sharp turn.

- I learned, through the arduous demands of campaigning, that I had more stamina than I had ever imagined. (A lesson in self-awareness)

- I learned to delegate tasks in my business in a manner that effectively freed my time and fully relied on staff expertise. (A lesson in trust)

- I learned to let go of "little stuff," those small items or concerns that unduly clutter time and consume energy. (A lesson in setting clear priorities)

- I learned the value of having a driver, a staff move that helped me maintain freshness and have far more time for thought and vital communications. (A lesson in strategic hiring. The driver I brought aboard during the campaign remains with me as a valuable personal asset in my business.)

My campaign "failed" in the sense that it did not lead me into elected office. But in terms of the professional and personal insights it provided, it was a stunning success. During the year I ventured outside my comfort zone via that sharp turn, business almost quadrupled. Both my staff and I grew in efficiency, attention to essentials, teamwork, timely decision-making, creativity, trust. I can emphatically state that it "turned out" to be a great growth experience.

## Paths of Exploration
(an expansion of action-points noted in chapter seven)

Here's a quick question: Would you rather be known as A) a dull, static and rigid person or as B) someone who is adventurous, dynamic and flexible. If you answered A), continue reading this chapter as my ardent attempt to convince you to alter your perspective. If you answered B), continue reading this chapter as words of encouragement and my strong endorsement of your choice. In either case, my goal is to help you move outside your comfort zone, to follow some of the innumerable "paths of exploration" that can enrich, energize and enlighten you every day of your life. In the segments that follow, I name just a few of the areas (although I have selected ones I believe to be central) in which you will find such life-enhancing paths. My suggestions sketch very briefly some ways of stepping forward.

**Food** -- Whatever your culinary preferences, add new items to the table! Discovering what folks in other places eat in fact gives you a taste of their culture. "You are what you eat," contains a core element of a broad truth. The foods that people eat, the ways they prepare and consume them, tells much about their environment and their social system. If you feel reluctant to engage your palate in exploration or assume you won't enjoy certain things, take the approach an acquaintance takes with her small children. When presenting a new food item, she has a rule (no matter the "that's yucky" or "I'm gonna hate it" protests): "You just have to take a try-it-bite." The children accept this instruction knowing that their response will be accepted. More often than not, that response is along the lines of, "Hey, this is pretty good." The key is to make the attempt, to get outside the comfort zone of customary cuisine. Personally and professionally as well, you will find many applications for the concept of "try-it-bites."

**Sports** -- There are obvious and well-documented benefits of physical activity. Whatever you choose to do in the realm of athletics -- Bravo! If you use your activity to maintain fitness, excellent. If you use it to engage in hearty competition, terrific. To find solitude… to enjoy social contacts… to relax… to have fun… all great. My urging is that you consider using athletics/physical activity as a means of disrupting your level of comfort in ways that prove challenging. Bodily benefits expand into ones that affect your entire being. Some examples: Those comfortable with solo activities can join a team. Those comfortable with group or team participation can find an individual sport. Those comfortable with ticking off short-term accomplishments can set a course focused on a long-term goal. Those inclined to be undisciplined can apply themselves to a supervised or monitored exercise regimen. Those accustomed to seeking an adrenaline rush can apply themselves to activities designed to induce calm. Sports/physical activities give us both immediate and ongoing affirmation of the fact that there are plenty of things that are enjoyable and good for us outside our comfort zone.

**Vacations/Travel** -- The most important part of taking a vacation is to embrace fully its basic purpose which is to vacate your office, business concerns and daily patterns. If you empty yourself of these things (Latin, vacatus, "emptied"), you make space for new and enriching experiences. Vacations/travels provide opportunities to put yourself and those with whom you journey into unfamiliar places and situations. I strongly recommend that you not allow vacations to become predictable or routine, mere minor expansions of your comfort zone. Traveling to new areas (for example, where you do not speak the language), trying new activities (for example, zip-lining or sketching or sport fishing), immersing in history (for example, visiting sites and learning a region's struggles and triumphs), exploring new cultures (for example, discovering the contributions of indigenous people), provide experiences to discuss and reflect upon when you return home. Also, almost always, the experiences shape you into being a more receptive, accepting person. I have consistently found that when I spend money to travel, I end up being enriched. And vacating my comfort zone fills me with fresh understandings.

**Music** -- Music has been called by some the language of the soul, and we have all experienced how music affects our emotions/moods. It's sheer pleasure to be able to listen to our favorite kinds of music, to find just the right pieces to suit an occasion or to mesh with our feelings. But I believe that exposing our ears to styles of music that we "can't stand" or "don't understand," that we have rejected or neglected, is something well worth trying. Getting outside our auditory comfort zone may enable us to bond with people on new emotional levels. Achieving a genuine depth of music appreciation means, in a way, becoming multi-lingual in the sense that we can understand the language of the soul in many forms. We will all find our own ways to expand our musical universe, but I will share one method that works for me. I simply select for my listening device a random playlist. New tones, new tunes, new and broader tastes.

**Issues and Ideas** -- It is enormously comfortable to hold fast to our own settled opinions on issues and to have a set filter for hearing the ideas of others. But this intellectual comfort zone is personally perilous and, as we interact with others, relationally deadly. Setting ourselves up as the arbiter of correctness or the source of wisdom is both decidedly arrogant and egregiously wrong. And we need to remember that education is a process to pursue and not a product we possess. It has also been noted by many that we can seek either wisdom or agreement, but we cannot assume the two are identical. A friend I consider wise has a compellingly comfort-puncturing practice. On every issue and on every expressed idea, he tries to set up his email to receive information from a full spectrum of resources… right-wing conservatives and radical leftists, evangelicals and atheists, flat-earthers and scientific researchers, etc. From information gathered, with humility and consideration, he shapes his opinions and responses. He, and we, grow when we accept evolving ideas and engaged dialogue as allies that help us escape the prison of an intellectual comfort zone. Only an open mind can receive new knowledge. I monitor my own open-mindedness by trying to take, from anything I consider a learning opportunity or experience, one idea that I commit to ponder and, if applicable, put into practice. That gives me a manageable focus. And as I reflect, I also remember that a fertile mind always craves the seeds of new ideas to nurture and to develop.

**Spirituality** -- This word conjures up a range of responses as wide as the horizon. My reason for bringing it up is to inspire you (I use that phrase intentionally!) to devote some attention (again, intentional) to your relationship with things beyond yourself. That's a broad statement meant to indicate my deep respect for the variety of ways that people address spiritual exploration. Individual practices. Communal gatherings. Readings. Meditation. Prayer. Pilgrimage. Dietary disciplines. Chants. Silence. And more…. Years ago, I heard someone described this way: "He considers himself a self-made man. The only problem is he worships his maker." Spirituality, in just about any form of expression, beckons us outside any tendency toward self-adulation and self-absorption, a seductive comfort zone that is both unhealthy and unappealing. Simply stated, I invite you to explore spirituality on your own terms and to develop an appreciation for the myriad ways people can engage in the quest for deeper understandings of goodness, grandeur, mystery and meaning.

I hope, as I've reviewed just a few areas of life where comfort zones can become entrapping or disabling, I've in some ways encouraged you to actions that are liberating and that move you toward making linear progress, taking a sharp turn or moving along paths of exploration.

"All right, Scott," you may be thinking, "I understand how breaking free of confining comfort zones can enhance and enrich my personal growth. But what's this got to do with my business success?!" I won't respond by saying, "Everything," but that's close to the truth. Let me share a story before a brief summary paragraph that answers the question directly and succinctly. Many years ago, a neighbor had a daffodil plant growing in a planter on his deck. The plant thrived, but my neighbor decided to replant the multiplying bulbs by a pond in his yard. Within a few years, daffodils ran all along the shore and my neighbor dug up bulbs to give to friends around town. Now, a couple decades later, the beauty of daffodils decorates numerous yards around the village each spring. That initial daffodil might have remained in its comfort zone on the deck and been tended in a way to keep it confined. Instead, its owner made a decision to let it grow and flourish and have a widespread positive impact. Your gifts and talents are like that original daffodil... be a wise owner and do not let your potential be a potted plant.

I'll close this chapter with just a couple observations that put this entire chapter in context. First, getting out of comfort zones is crucial to business success because it gets you accustomed to pushing beyond perceived limits – you will develop your capacity to exceed expectations. And second, every time you step out of your comfort zones, you create new opportunities to find points of contact with other persons – you will expand your potential client base.

So, I invite you to break out of your comfort zones with courage and commitment and a bit of joyful enthusiasm! Consider doing so as central to your success. The rewards can be stunning. I've come to appreciate that deeply, and I assure you that, **if I can do it, you can, too.**

# 12. "What Are You Going to Do?"

The title of this chapter, "What Are You Going to Do?" frames a question that is at the core of your career and your life. My reason for writing this book is not to pad my resume (I hope I've grown beyond that!) or to draw attention to a "see what I have done" presentation of personal history. My intent is simple: to offer materials and insights that can lead you to achieve satisfaction/success both in your business career and in your life beyond the business context. As I've noted before about contacts with clients – it's about them – so with this chapter. It's not about me – it's about you. Thus far, you've read through the substance of this book. Thanks! I hope you have persisted because you find my thoughts, insights, observations and tips both challenging and substantive. I offer them humbly as a mentor, not a master. Now it's up to you to act upon those things you have determined to be of value.

Please notice that I did not ask you to decide what you were going to do with the materials in this book. There is an old riddle that states: "There were three frogs sitting on a log. One decided to jump off. How many were left?" The correct answer is three... the point being that making a decision is quite different from taking action.

"So what can I do?" you ask. Plenty! Here are a few suggestions to get started. First and foremost comes a firm decision to commit to the belief that intent becomes transformative only when ideas take life as actions.

A. I can adopt a new approach to how I deal with people or issues:

> ... pick one skill or technique that is either new to you or something you have neglected. Practice it until it feels natural, until it truly

becomes part of you. Then move on to another technique or skill. Aim for consistency and proficiency – not everything at once! Trust in the power of sequential progress.

B. I can strengthen my business health with the exercise of personal choice and resolve:

... choose prospects and get clients who are aligned with your own moral and social beliefs. Although you must recognize that everyone is a potential client and everyone merits thorough professional service, it is wise to build a cache of clients with whom you have significant values and goals in common. Choosing to focus on those with whom you have a positive level of personal comfort is mutually beneficial. Good matches matter and it is uplifting to feel that you and your client are truly collaborators reaching a shared goal.

C. I can incorporate three or four insights from this book into my business and personal life:

... select those things that just stuck in your memory as good ideas, that resonated with your experience. Write them down, repeat them daily, let them become part of the fiber of your life.

D. I can set up a self-monitoring system:

... commit to a scheduled/structured program of self-evaluation. At fixed intervals (every six weeks is a good starting point) and in a comfortable location, review what you are working on and ask: "Did I accomplish my goals or not? What changes do I need to make?" Review, too, how you are dealing with the opportunities and demands of your job and ask: "Am I keeping track of my number of calls, my prospect contacts, my yes/no responses? What is my average size case? Is my data base up to date and easy to use? Are any changes needed in office procedures?" The mirror of regular honest self-assessment provides a picture you can get nowhere else.

E. I can, as an extension of D), find a trusted companion who will hold me accountable:

... select someone who cares about you, speaks directly, knows the essentials of your work. Meet a couple times a year with this person to review past activity and set forth future plans. The ideal person to have as your "accountability companion" is someone who is both fervent in validating on-target ideas and dedicated in challenging goals or actions, someone who is both compassionate in hearing annoyances and confident in providing a different perspective. I have felt comfortable having a trusted friend fill this role for me but I recognize that some may feel it more effective to hire a business coach. Whatever works best!

F. I can focus on my abilities rather than my disabilities:

... dream big and develop your gifts. You remember, I'm quite sure, from the beginning of this book, that I was born with serious and limiting eye problems that affected my social and educational development. Even after the operation that improved my eyesight and even after contact lenses replaced glasses, I still felt scarred by years of living with that disability, with being told what I couldn't do because of it. I contend that all of us have disabilities, things that hamper or hinder our peak performance. Sometimes these are obvious to us and sometimes they get instilled in us by the diagnoses and judgments of others. My firm belief about disabilities of any kind is that we can succumb to them or overcome them. We can become defined by our disabilities or we can cultivate our abilities. And sometimes – this is key, I think – our disabilities generate gifts we can develop. Out of the disability of poor eyesight I developed the gift of insight grounded in careful listening. Out of the disability of partial blindness I developed the gift of clear vision for how I might best use my talents.

As a closing comment in this final, "So what can I do?" suggestion, I want to encourage you to read the life-stories of people you consider great or admirable. You will often find that their achievements derived from what they overcame… and so, I believe, it is with all of us. Beethoven overcame deafness in his later years to produce world-renowned music. Einstein overcame the designation of being a "slow child" to become perhaps the greatest mathematical genius in all history. Jackie Robinson overcame a culture of prejudice to reach the Baseball Hall of Fame. Helen Keller overcame blindness and deafness to become a messenger of hope and inspiration. Stephen Hawking overcame ALS to speak as a voice that described our universe. Whatever disability you identify in yourself can be viewed as a stumbling block that impedes success or as a hurdle that, when overcome, opens a path to achievement.

### Discern, define and develop your abilities.

A friend of mine has a young daughter who is at the age of rapid language acquisition, a time when children experiment with usage and try out words and phrases. He told me that whenever she gave someone a gift, she'd say, "I give this for you," rather than the standard, "I give this to you." He couldn't, in any way, figure out what was wrong with the way his daughter described her giving. "Then," he said, "I figured out why her way might be better!" He noted that giving something to someone sounds rather mechanical, the simple task of transferring something from one person to another. Giving that is for someone implies a thoughtful personal investment, a hope that the gift will be useful and meaningful.

In wrapping up this book, I realize that my intent, in relation to those of you who became my readers, is to give it for you. It is my sincere hope that you receive from it materials that inspire you to act in ways that enhance your career and bring a new fullness to your life. And I'll affirm once more what I have stated at the close of every chapter, my heartfelt belief that **if I can do it, you can, too!**

# Appendix

An appendix to a book (from Latin, appendere, "an addition, continuation something attached") is intended to provide readers with helpful supplementary material. This, or any other book, is essentially complete without an appendix and it's an author's option to offer one or not. I choose to do so in service to A) expressing my hopes for how you use this book, B) offering a quick and concise review in the form of "takeaways," and C) extending a bit of a challenge.

A. My primary goal in putting this book together is to create a resource that presents an holistic approach to sales and to life in general. And so, I'll share my four firm hopes related to mind, heart, body and spirit/energy....

1. I hope you will keep in <u>mind</u> the takeaways provided in this appendix. They can keep you mentally sharp and help shape your thought processes.

2. I hope you will take to <u>heart</u> the suggestions for shaping a lifestyle that enhances both business success and personal relationship. The takeaways are also things to keep close and accessible within yourself.

3. I hope you will <u>embody</u> the materials you find most useful in the daily practices of your business. Consider the takeaways as exercises designed to strengthen the body of work that is your professional life.

4. I hope you have found this book <u>inspiring</u> and <u>energizing</u>. The takeaways serve as ready resources to spark your recollection of its basic contents.

B. A review of the book's contents…

The takeaways are my attempt to distill the message of the book into what I consider essentials. They are intended to send you back to the designated chapters and to prompt your recollections and re-explorations of what you discovered there. In effect, the takeaways are a précis of the book; they summarize but do not include specifics.

C. A challenge…

In writing this book, I have made the bold presumption that I have something valuable to offer you. Yet I am also humbly aware that I have taken on the role of educator, literally one who "draws forth" what others have within.

I freely acknowledge that what I've set before you may elicit insights, understandings and questions that were not part of my own thought process. But that's wonderful! A friend of mine who has been a motivational speaker for decades once told me this:

"At the close of my speaking engagements, I would regularly have people come up to me to tell me what particular message they heard that had an impact upon them. Often, what they identified seemed to have little, tangential or no relation to what I intended as my meaning. Initially, I protested or tried to correct my listeners' understandings. And then, I recognized that it was both arrogant and unhelpful to assume that what I intended was more important than what people found significant. So I began simply thanking folks. If they discovered something meaningful and positive in what I said, who was I to contradict?!"

So with the takeaways. And that is why I've included two blank lines after my own suggested emphases. As you bring your unique set of experiences and perspectives into interaction with what I've written, you will gain understandings I could not have imagined. I challenge you to come up with a couple ideas or guides to action inspired by each chapter. These are things you can own and can adopt as personal resolutions/commitments.

Identify your own hopes and work to realize them. Review the contents of this book from time to time with the goal of gaining fresh, useful insights. And as you form these, accept the challenge of creating your own set of takeaways that can enhance your business practices and personal life.

## Takeaways

#1. "No Magic"

> Success in sales and service is not based on any magic, but rather on belief in one's own developed skills, dedication and innate abilities.

> Keep your tools-of-the-trade sharp, hone your techniques to suit your personal style, and regard every client contact as a practice session for getting better at what you do.

> Since there's no magic involved, be entirely open and up-front with your clients.

> —

> —

#2. "Humility"

> Only by being humble and grounded can you truly give priority position to your client's hopes, goals, interests and well-being.

> Humility is both an attractive personal trait and the enabler of true partnerships (personal and business).

Humility gives us a lens for examining how our actions affect others.

There is no downside to practicing genuine humility.

—

—

## #3. "Listening"

Recognize that listening is a skill to be developed, a skill with enough rarity to make it immensely valuable.

Remove your own agenda from the activity of careful listening, and make sure you are not formulating a response before you hear fully what is being said.

Ask questions of others on the basis of what you truly want/need to know.

—

—

## #4. "Hard Work"

It is possible to work too much (measured in time); it is not possible to work too hard (measured in effort, energy, dedication and application of skills).

Whatever your job or task-at-hand, it merits the best you have to offer.

Hard work always teaches a lesson. Be alert to this by defining, assessing and, if possible, applying what you learned.

—

—

## #5. "Gut Instinct"

Identify times in your life when following gut instinct proved beneficial, and be alert to common features of these occasions.

Define your own preferred balance of heeding gut instinct and accumulating advice/analysis; remember that acting on the basis of this balance can be tempered by time.

There is significant scientific evidence for trusting gut instinct.

—

—

## #6. "Always Selling"

There is nothing more crucial to success in sales than establishing, nurturing and maintaining a reputation for honesty and competence.

Focus on the "Six A's." Commit to developing your reputation by being: approachable, alert, accommodating, assertive, attentive and appreciative.

"Always selling" is an opportunity, not a burden.

—

—

#7. "Balance"

Pay attention to the balance-point pairings of: acquisition-dispersal, interaction-solitude, organization-exploration, business-beyond. Try to define and describe activities in your life within each pairing.

It is crucial – personally and professionally – that you discern what equilibrium means and feels like.

When you find/identify a balance-point in your life, you will sense an inner stability. Hold it and claim it and commit yourself to embodying its components.

—

—

#8. "Everyone a Potential Client… or a Source of Inspiration"

Never write off a person as a potential client; improbables can become impressive surprises.

Be alert to personal connections of clients that may link you to others. Preparation and alertness in this matter are keys to opportunity.

Cultivate, in relation to clients, the attributes of persistence, openness, genuine interest and willingness to meet needs.

—

—

#9.  "Investing in Dividends Pays People… Investing in People Pays Dividends"

When evaluating investment strategies, look carefully and openly at DRIPs. There is little downside long-term and considerable upside.

Your investments in staff are crucial and merit intensive, ongoing attention.

Invest in yourself by using a variety of means to become better at what you do.

—

—

#10. "Essentials"

Pay attention to how to be with clients as a competent advisor, concerned listener and friend.

Clients and staff need to know how and when you are present for them… who you are, what you offer them, how you conduct your business, when you are accessible, what your expertise can provide.

Simply – be your best self… for yourself, loved ones, clients, everyone.

—

—

#11. "Get Out of Your Comfort Zone"

Comfort zones can be cages that inhibit or prohibit growth-enhancing exploration.

Review your life history and note times when moving outside your comfort zone led to positive results. Identify what prompted/inspired such moves.

Target areas of life for adventurous exploration/expansion (for example: foods, travel, issue research, spirituality, athletics, hobbies, etc.).

—

—

#12. "What Are You Going to Do?"

One at a time, with earnest and enthusiastic effort, adopt each "can do" suggestion listed in this brief chapter.

—

—